Reaching Teenagers

Practical Bible
Methods for The
Local Church Youth Ministry

Dr. Don Woodard

All Scriptures quotations are from the King James Bible

LightKeeper Publications
PO Box 490
Troutville, VA 24175
540-354-8573
Csm2va@netzero.net

ISBN: 1463774699
ISBN-13:9781463774691

DEDICATION

To Mrs. Georgia Parish

March 17, 1917 ~ April 6, 2011

Thank you for taking me to Sunday school when I was five years old, for being a soul winner, a Sunday school teacher, and a Faithful servant of the Lord Jesus Christ.

"For God is not unrighteous to forget your work and labor of love, which ye have shewed toward his name, in that ye have ministered to the saints, and do minister."

Hebrews 6:10

Dear Wayne:

I kept my promise.

Don

CONTENTS

Foreword

The book you hold in your hand is one of a kind. This book, *Reaching Teenagers,* will help to fill a great void in fundamental Christianity. Dr. Woodard writes from experience and with a desire to see America's young people have victory in their life and serve God. This book is an excellent resource in three aspects. *First,* it is a good tool for strengthening an existing youth ministry. *Second,* this book is an excellent resource for Church planters and new youth leaders in starting a youth ministry from scratch. *Third,* this book is rich in ideas and principles for reviving a stagnant youth ministry.

I have known Don Woodard for several years and he has proved himself to be faithful. As God's man, he has been faithful to the Word of God, fervent in reaching and building young people, and fearless in defending the faith.

Every Pastor, Youth Pastor, and Church planter in America ought to have this book. It contains a wealth of valuable material. On every page you will find great truths and principles that will help you minister to young people.

I heartily recommend this book.

Dr. Glen Spencer Jr., Pastor

Vernon Baptist Church
Tunkhannock, PA

The Harvest Truly is Plenteous

"The diseased have ye not strengthened, neither have ye healed that which was sick, neither have ye bound up that which was broken, neither have ye brought again that which was driven away, neither have ye sought that which was lost; but with force and with cruelty have ye ruled them.

And they were scattered, because there is no shepherd: and they became meat to all the beasts of the field, when they were scattered. My sheep wandered through all the mountains, and upon every high hill: yea, my flock was scattered upon all the face of the earth, and none did search or seek after them. Therefore, ye shepherds, hear the word of the Lord;" Ezekiel 34:4-7

"When he saw the multitudes, he was moved with compassion on them, because they fainted and were scattered abroad, as sheep having no shepherd. Then saith he unto his disciples, The harvest truly is plenteous, but the labourers are few; Pray ye therefore the Lord of the harvest, that he will send forth labourers into his harvest."

Matthew 9:36-38

You don't have to look far to see that there is a need for the local New Testament Church to reach young people with the message of hope that is in Jesus Christ. The following statistics should convince us and burden us that the harvest truly is plenteous and that the need for Local New Testament Churches to reach young people with the gospel in America is crucial and urgent.

Suicide

[1]Every year, thousands of youth die in North America, not from cancer or car accidents, but by their own hand. They make the choice that they want to die, and they take their own life. Statistics show that suicide is the third leading cause of death among those 15 to 25 years of age, and it is the sixth leading cause of death among those 5 to 14 years of age. It is estimated that 500,000 teenagers try to kill themselves every year, and about 5,000 succeed. 5,000, that is right up there with cancer and homicide.

Facts about Suicide

• There is an 80% chance that someone who has attempted suicide will try to kill themselves again.

• 8 out of 10 people who commit suicide give clues that they wanted to kill themselves.

• 500,000 teenagers aged 15 to 25 tries to kill themselves every year.

• Over 5,000 teenagers commit suicide each year.

• People who kill themselves usually don't want to die; they just want to get away from the pain.

• In the United States more people kill themselves than are killed by other people.

• Most people who kill themselves do not leave notes.

---

[1] The American Academy of Child and Adolescent Psychiatry.

• Teenage guys kill themselves two times more than anyone else does.

• Clusters of teenage suicides have been occurring more often, this is when one suicide triggers many others in the same area.

[2]Facts about Alcohol and Teens

• It has been estimated that over three million teenagers are out-and-out alcoholics. Several million more have a serious drinking problem that they cannot manage on their own.

• Boys whose fathers are anti-social alcoholics are more likely to perform worse intellectually, cognitively and academically than their peers.

• Young people who take up alcohol drinking before age fifteen are four times more likely to become alcohol dependent.

• Alcohol use is involved in one-half of all murders, accidental deaths, and suicides, and one half of all crimes.

• Alcohol kills 6.5 times more youth than all other illicit drugs combined.

• Alcohol use is the number one drug problem among young people.

• Advertisers spend more than $1 billion each year on alcohol advertisements.

• 4.4 Million College students are binge drinkers and another 1.89 million are heavy drinkers.

---

[2] Focus on Adolescent Services

• 75 percent of young teens say that alcohol is easy to acquire. Approximately two-thirds of teenagers who drink report that they buy their own alcohol.

• Underage drinking cost the United States more than $53 Billion every year, enough to buy every public school student a state-of-the-art computer.

• During a typical weekend, an average of one teenager (age15-20) dies each hour in a car crash. More than forty-five percent of those crashes involve alcohol.

• 2.6 Million teenagers don't know that a person can die from an alcohol overdose.

• In 1998, about 10.4 million drinkers in the United States were less than 21 years old.

• Forty percent of network TV episodes made drinking look like a positive experience.

• Sixty percent of college women diagnosed with a sexually transmitted disease were drunk at the time of infection.

[3]Teen Pregnancy

• The United States has the highest teenage pregnancy rate of all developed countries.

• About One Million teenagers become pregnant each year; 95% of those pregnancies are unintended, and almost one third end in abortions.

• Public cost from teenage childbearing totaled $120 billion from 1985-1990.

---

[3] National Center for Chronic Disease Prevention and Health Promotion

• Birth rates among teenagers vary from state to state; some states have rates almost three times higher than those of the states with the lower rates.

[4]Teen Drug Abuse

• In 1998 22% of all eighth-graders and 49% of all twelfth graders said they had tried marijuana.

• In 1998 40% of eighth-graders did not see a great risk in regular use of LSD

• Use of illicit drugs by twelfth-graders climbed from 21.1% in 1992 to 42.4% in 1997.

• Marijuana use among teenage girls is increasing faster than it is among boys; girls' drug violations also increased by more than 13,000 from 1991 to 1996, most of which were for possession of marijuana.

[5]• In 2000 54% of High school seniors said they have experimented with illicit drugs. 48.8% had experimented with marijuana and 14.2% said they had experimented with inhalants.

The Fatherless

[6]• 85% of all children that exhibit behavioral disorders come from fatherless homes.

[7]• 90% of all homeless and runaway children are from fatherless homes.

[8]• 71% of all high school dropouts come from fatherless homes.

---

[4] PBS Homepage
[5] National Institute on Drug Abuse
[6] National Institute on Drug Abuse
[7] Center for Disease Control

[9]• 63% of youth suicides are from fatherless homes.

[10]• 80% of rapists with displaced anger come from fatherless homes.

[11]• 85% of all youths sitting in prisons grew up in a fatherless home.

[12]• "Daughters of single parents are 53% more likely to marry as teenagers, 164% more likely to have a premarital birth, and 92% more likely to dissolve their own marriages."

[13]• 71% of teenage pregnancies are to children of single parents.

[14]• Eighteen million children live in single parent homes.

[15]• 24 Million Children live without their biological father.

Dear friend, put a face with these statistics, these are young people in our towns, maybe even our relatives, they have souls, they are lives who need to be reached for Jesus Christ; these statistics should move us to compassion. We have not taken a close look at abortion, violence or the teen runaway problem in the United States and yet the statistics we have listed are alarming.

The Local New Testament Church cannot look away from the plight of our young people any longer.

---

[8] National Principals Association
[9] Bureau of Census
[10] Criminal Justice and Behavior
[11] Texas Department of Corrections
[12] Barbara Defoe Whitehead
[13] US Department of Health and Human Services
[14] National Fatherhood Institute
[15] National Fatherhood Facts and Statistics

In Matthew 9:36 Jesus saw the multitude and was moved with compassion. It is time for us to look on the multitude, to see the destruction of our young people for the reality that it is.

We can no longer close our eyes to the needs of young people in America; we can no longer shift the responsibility to the government, the public school system or community social programs. The Great Commission was given to the Local New Testament Church, not to government agencies. We must see the multitude of young people who need Christ and we must move to action while the harvest truly is plenteous, *"while it is day: the night cometh, when no man can work."* (John 9:4b)

The Great Commission And The Local Church Youth Ministry

"And Jesus came and spake unto them, saying, All power is given unto me in heaven and in earth. Go ye therefore, and teach all nations, baptizing them in the name of the Father, and of the Son, and of the Holy Ghost: Teaching them to observe all things whatsoever I have commanded you: and, lo, I am with you alway, even unto the end of the world. Amen." Matthew 28:18-20

The Great Commission was given to the New Testament Church, in it the church is instructed to *"teach all nations"* in Mark 16:15 the Bible says, *"Go ye into all the world, and preach the gospel to every creature."* In Acts 1:8 Jesus again commissions the church, *"But ye shall receive power, after that the Holy Ghost is come upon you: and ye shall be witnesses unto me both in Jerusalem, and in all Judea, and in Samaria, and unto the uttermost part of the earth."* From these passages of Scripture we must conclude that in fulfilling the Great Commission we are to go to all peoples of all races, of all customs, meeting their need to receive the gospel and teaching converts to observe all things. *"All nations", "All the world"* and *"to every creature"*, includes the teenagers in our Jerusalem (local community). We are to take the gospel to them and we are to minister to them.

Notice the word *"both"* used in Acts 1:8, this implies that the local church is to be involved in all four areas simultaneously. If all we are doing is sending missionaries to the uttermost, then we are being helpful, but we are not fulfilling the Great Commission because we do not have it in balance. If all we are doing is seeking to reach the fair-haired upper class adults in our Jerusalem (local community), then we are being helpful, but we are not fulfilling the Great Commission and we do not have it in balance.

The Great Commission in balance is the Local New Testament Church reaching out to everyone they can in every area possible with the Gospel of Jesus Christ and ministering to the needs of people; including the teenagers in our Jerusalem.

The word minister or ministry means to serve, to aid, to supply thing's necessary. Young people have needs; the problems, temptations and challenges they face today in our society are greater and viler than ever in our history. Many young people today have broken homes, broken hearts and broken spirits. They are lost without Christ, they have spiritual, social and emotional needs; according to the Great Commission, the New Testament Church is to minister to those needs.

America has twenty seven million teenagers; millions of which are addicted to drugs, alcohol, pornography; some are abused through incest, abused physically and spiritually. There are millions of teenagers in witchcraft and Satan worship, the need for our churches to have a ministry of reaching teenagers is momentous. And yet the teenagers of America is one to the world's most un-pursued mission fields. Add to the un-pursued, the teens who attend our churches, some attend with their families, some with friends, some because of the bus ministry.

Others attend simply because people such as a youth leader, Sunday school teacher, or pastor cares for them.

These young people also have needs that a local church youth ministry can provide for. Then we have the teenage sons and daughters of our pastors, missionaries and Christian workers, who also have needs.

The assignment given to the Local New Testament Church in the Great Commission is to reach people with the gospel of Jesus Christ and then to disciple those, so they will reach people with the gospel of Jesus Christ and disciple their converts. This is done through ministering to the needs of people, through meeting people's basic needs to be loved, cared for, given hope and a purpose for living. In order for a local New Testament church to reach teenagers it must have a ministry to teenagers, it must serve, aid, and supply things necessary.

The church must minister to all young people, the alcoholic, the drug addict, the pregnant teenage girl, the preacher's son, the alcoholic's son, and the fatherless. Many churches today have convinced themselves that if they have a handful of teens attend an amusement park each summer, share a "Bible devotion" and call it a youth group, then they have accomplished something in reaching teenagers in America for the cause of Christ. The truth is that we would be far more effective in reaching teenagers if we would forget about a "youth group" and focus on our churches having a structured <u>ministry</u> to the young people in our community.

If our churches will apply the principles of the Great Commission in ministering to the needs of America's teenagers; loving them, caring for them, challenging and encouraging them to serve the Lord. We will then have a large group of young people that will have victory in their lives and will achieve great things for the cause of Christ. Youth groups entertain teenagers, but youth ministries supply things necessary for strong Bible character, compassion, victory, and steadfastness. Although the problems teens face today are bigger and more vile than that of thirty years ago; the same Bible principles and methods used thirty years ago to establish strong New Testament Church youth ministries, can still work today. The purpose of this thesis is to share ideas, principles, and philosophies about developing an effective youth ministry within the local New Testament Church.

As you begin to read through these ideas and principles please put yourself in the mind-set of having a youth ministry for the young people in your Jerusalem.

Teenagers and Their Needs

"For I was an hungered, and ye gave me meat: I was thirsty, and ye gave me drink: I was a stranger, and ye took me in: Naked and ye clothed me: I was sick, and ye visited me: I was in prison, and ye came unto me."

Matthew 25:35-36

In this passage of scripture The Lord Jesus Christ shares a lesson in the Olivet discourse on the great commission; that lesson is about caring for and meeting the needs of people.

A church youth ministry that is founded on the great commission in meeting the needs that young people have will be strong and spiritually fruitful. A youth ministry founded on entertainment and emotion will be carnal and not spiritually fruitful. You can always draw a crowd of people with pizza and ice cream; and I am not against compelling young people to church activities, as we will discuss later. But after the refreshments, how many go soul-winning, how many have a prayer life, and what spiritual victory do they have in their life because the Word of God was magnified in the meeting?

Young people can go anywhere for better or different entertainment, but you can't get genuine love just anywhere. You can't get hope through entertainment, and pizza and ice cream do not satisfy the emotional and spiritual needs young people have. In Matthew 25:35-36 Jesus speaks of hunger, thirst, nakedness, sickness and imprisonment. These are physical needs used to describe spiritual and emotional needs. Just as you and I have physical needs for food, water and rest.

We have spiritual needs as well, for we are body, mind, and spirit. We can learn from Jesus' discourse about fulfilling the physical, mental, and spiritual needs of people both young and old.

As we discussed earlier the word minister or ministry means to serve, to aid, to supply things necessary. By using Matthew 25:35-36 let us study the needs of teenagers that we may be able to better minister to them.

1) The Need to be Loved.

"I was an hungered, and ye gave me meat."

The word "hungered" is defined as starving, indigent, to toil for daily sustenance, distressed. Physically we must have food to sustain us; food satisfies a basic physical need. Emotionally people of all ages hunger for love. Knowing someone loves us helps to sustain us, to be loved is a basic emotional need.

Love has been distorted by the Hollywood movie makers, and by the Rock music culture; young people today are confused about what real love is. It appears that fear has replaced love in our society among our teens today. [16]Dr. Jay E. Adams, a noted Bible counselor, says in his book [17]The Christian Counselors Manual, "Fear and love vary inversely. The more fear the less love; the more love the less fear." First John 4:18 says, *"There is no fear in love; but perfect love casteth out fear: because fear hath torment. He that feareth is not made perfect in love."*

---

[16] Author, Lecturer, Bible counselor

[17] Presbyterian and Reformed Publishing Company

Every day in our society teenage girls become pregnant out of wedlock, have abortions; young men act out their anger, bitterness, hatred, depression, rage, and insecurities through drug abuse, alcohol and violence. Because when there is a lack of love there is an abundance of fear and *"fear hath torment"*. All of this is done seeking to fulfill the emotional need to be loved; teens are looking for someone to love them. Love takes away fear and replaces it with assurance, peace, hope and forgiveness. For many young people, having the assurance that someone loves them could make all the difference in the world.

2) The Need for Truth

"I was thirsty, and ye gave me drink."

Teenagers today have a spiritual thirst, a thirst for truth. In our society abortion, drugs, immorality, the rock culture, Hollywood lifestyles, Planned Parenthood and humanistic philosophies have deceived young people. The Apostle Paul wrote in Philippians 3:2 *"Beware of dogs, beware of evil workers, beware of the concision."* The word "dogs," is used figuratively referring to someone that takes a lie and tries to make it a truth. Many of our teenagers have been fed lies until they believe them; unfortunately those lies have brought a lot of heartache and despair to our teens.

Modern psychiatry has told our young people that the way to deal with hurt and anger is to throw a foam rubber brick against the wall or to channel your bitterness and anger to another area of life; or to get on mind altering medication. Medication does not solve spiritual problems and they do not fill the void of love or the emptiness of lies. These things only lead to more emptiness, hopelessness, despair and anger. The Bible teaches us to forgive the one we are bitter toward. Victory and closure comes through prayer and forgiveness. Hosea 4:6 says, *"My people are destroyed for lack of knowledge."* Every day in America our teenagers lives are destroyed from a lack of knowing the truth. The deceit and destruction of Satan has bound them to sin. But Jesus said in John 8:32 *"And ye shall know the truth, and the truth shall make you free."* Teenagers need the truth of the gospel of Jesus Christ; they need to know the truth of his grace and salvation, that they may know the hope and joy of his forgiveness. They are looking for the truth and those of us who hold to the eternal Word of God have it, and we must get the truth to them.

3) The Need for Commitment

"...ye gave me"

The word "gave" in the statement *"ye gave me meat"* has a similar yet different meaning from the statement *"ye gave me drink"*. In the statement *"ye gave me meat"* the word *"gave"* is defined as, bestow, bring forth, commit, deliver up, give, grant, minister, and offer; whereas the statement, *"ye gave me drink"* literally means to furnish drink.

Commitment is a word that is lacking in our society today. Many men do not make commitments to the women who bare them children. Many parents are not committed to their children and may I say that far too many fathers are not committed to their families. I remind you of three words in our definition of the word *"gave"*; bestow, commit and minister. In Jesus statement, *"ye gave me"* he was saying I had a need and you were committed to meeting my need. I was hungry and you were committed to giving me meat. I was thirsty and you were committed to giving me drink.

Teenagers today are looking for someone that is committed to helping them with their needs in life and to answer the questions they have. They are not concerned with how much knowledge you have; what your income level is, or your level on the social ladder. But your level of commitment in meeting their needs will impress them!

Will you be committed to them when they are struggling with family problems? Will you be committed to them when they go astray, and will you be committed enough to go after them? Will you be committed to them when they are striving for victory over drugs, alcohol, anger, bitterness or depression? Will you be committed enough to cheer for them when they try, yet stumble? Will you be committed to them when your phone rings at four o'clock in the morning and they need someone to talk to? Committed leadership is an important need that our young people have today, a need that does not require any talent, prestige, education, or money to provide! Only character, compassion and effort are needed. But expressing commitment can make all the difference in their lives.

4) The Need for Leadership

"I was a stranger and ye took me in."

The statement "I was a stranger", describes very well the need teenagers have for leadership today. The word "stranger" in this passage is defined figuratively as being a novice. It is one who is not clear of what to do or where to go, one who is in unfamiliar territory.

The statement, "ye took me in" defines the fulfillment of the need for leadership. The word "took" means, to gather, to collect, to assemble, and to lead. I submit to you that teenagers assemble at rock concerts, in gangs, and in bad company looking for leadership. Everyone is following someone, we all have our heroes, and we have leaders in our lives from which, we glean strength and security.

Many of our teenagers look to movie stars, rock musicians and athletic stars for leadership and inspiration. They see these people as being successful at what they do. Although we as Bible believing Christians do not agree with the rock culture or the life styles of many professional athletes, based on the world's standards and in the minds of many teens they are successful.

Teenagers need Christian leaders who are an example of "success" in the Christian life, and a success in their profession. Leaders who are victorious in their own battles of bitterness, anger, depression and despairing circumstances.

We all need leaders that lead by example, by faith and confidence; by truth and prayer; by trying and trying again, and by victory. Teenagers want to follow success not failure, confidence not doubt, truth not lies or maybes, hope not uncertainty, and victory, not defeat.

Young people are strangers, in unfamiliar territory, not clear of what to do or where to go, and they are in need of leadership.

5) The Need for Vision

"Naked, and ye clothed me."

Here again our Saviour uses a word describing a spiritual or emotional need with a physical metaphor. The word "naked" means to be without covering, with torn garments. Spiritually, it is our carnal condition, Isaiah 64:6 says, "...all our righteousnesses are as filthy rags." Jesus made the statement, "...and ye clothed me." The word clothed is, to put on, to array to invest. Proverbs

29:18 says, "Where there is no vision, the people perish:" To have a vision for teenagers is to see them for what they can become, not for what they are. We are all sinners deserving of eternal punishment in Hell; but Jesus looked out from Calvary and saw us for what we could become. Without Christ we are without covering, we are naked spiritually; at best all we have of ourselves are as filthy rags. Jesus Christ sees us for what we can become not for what we are. He has a vision for us, He has goals and ambitions for our lives, and he sees us reaching a higher level of our potential. He does not see just our nakedness; He sees us arrayed in His righteousness.

When we look upon teenagers we must look beyond their spiritual nakedness and see them arrayed in the potential that they can have in Christ. We must invest in them. We must see them reaching a higher level of potential; then we must encourage them to strive in doing something great with their lives. Most teenagers will not see themselves becoming more than their leadership envisions, challenges and encourages them to become. Teenagers need vision; leadership who will see them for what they can be, not for what they are.

6) The Need for Hope

"I was sick and ye visited me."

Our world is filled with people who have no hope, a common note left by teenagers who commit suicide says something like, "My future holds no hope." Many teenagers today, are spiritually sick, feeble, weak, and they feel that there is no hope for them. They have put their trust in drugs, alcohol, immorality, friends, and even family only to be let down and come up empty handed and empty hearted.

We all want hope; we hope for good health; we hope our marriages will be happy ones; we hope our children will do well; we hope life will be long and prosperous for ourselves, and for the people we love.

Teenagers want hope, they want life to be joyful, they hope their family problems will go away, they hope they will succeed in school, and they hope their friendships will last. Jesus said, "...ye visited me" To visit means to look upon, to care for, to help. When a teenager knows he has parents, or a pastor, youth leader, and a church that looks after him and is there to help and give direction with compassion and genuine interest in their life, it strengthens their hope.

Hope gives security and security gives confidence and confidence produces victory. When a teenager is striving to live the Christian life in this demonic world; knowing someone cares and is cheering them on can make all the difference in their life.

7) The Need for Security

"I was in prison and ye came unto me."

For several years now I have gone into juvenile prisons to preach in chapel services and revival meetings. Our country has thousands of teenagers incarcerated in correctional facilities. I have also met hundreds of teenagers across America in a different kind of prison. They are imprisoned by Satan's strong holds; they live in a world of uncertainty. Their family lives are unstable, many of their friends are disloyal, and their days are filled with adversity. Jesus said concerning being in prison, "and ye came unto me." Notice he said of being sick, "ye visited me" but of prison he said, "ye came unto me". The word "came" implies to be present with. I believe one of the most important things a teenager needs in his or her life is security. A teenager that has Christian parents who are married to one another, rearing their children together, providing for their children spiritually and emotionally is much more stable than the teenager who comes from a broken home with lost parents who do not provide emotionally and spiritually. Society even proves it. Teenagers from a Christian home need the security of a good local church pastor, youth ministry, and youth leader to help reinforce what is taught at home and to provide the security that they are not the only Christian teenager in the world.

The teenagers from a broken home or those that have other family problems need the security of a good local church pastor, youth ministry, and youth leader. Because in going through the teen years we need to know that someone is present with us, to be assured that we are not alone.

There are four things that I believe are hindering our churches from establishing effective youth ministries.

1) Pastors that do not stay long in a church.

2) Pastors that do not have a concern for the young people in their area and who do not try to reach out to them.

3) Churches who are continually rotating people in the leadership position of the youth ministry.

4) Pastors and church leadership who lack vision.

Good leadership provides security; this cannot be accomplished if leadership is constantly changing. A youth leader that is going to develop an effective, strong and vibrant youth ministry must be faithful to the teenagers he serves.

The teenagers must have confidence that their youth leader is going to be "present with them" every week, at each activity, in each defeat, and at every victory. I can sum up giving teenagers in your youth ministry security in four words; "be there for them!"

Another area of security that is extremely important is in doctrine and principles. The Bible does not change and so doctrine never changes. And principles do not change; I have seen several churches go downhill quickly because they compromised on doctrine, principles and standards. If standards are compromised, then they are compromised at the level of leadership, when leadership compromises the security of the people is weakened.

If God ever did change his doctrine about salvation by grace, or if he changed his doctrine of eternal security we would suffer a loss of faith, our security in him would be weakened. (Praise God he does not change!) Teenagers look to leadership for security, we point them to Christ but they also have a certain level of their faith that rests on us. When we compromise principles, standards and doctrine, their faith is shaken; their security is weakened.

Teenagers need security and leadership must provide it. *"In as much as ye have done it unto one of the least of these my brethren, ye have done it unto me."* Matthew 25:40b

Teenage Group Characteristics

12-14 Year Olds

- Have moved from fantasy to realistic focus of life goals.
- Tend to reject ready-made solutions from adults in favor of their own.
- Are interested in activities involving the opposite sex. Learning to deal with the opposite sex.
- Experience rapid change in physical appearance.
- Concerned about developing and emerging sexuality.
- Challenge assumptions and question family values, abandon views of adults as all-powerful.
- Are able to think abstractly and hypothetically. Can think about thinking.
- Are ready for in-depth long-term experiences.
- Strive for independence yet want and need adults' help.
- Looking more to peers than adults. Seek peer recognition.
- Exhibit wide range of sexual maturity and growth patterns.

15-18 Year Olds

- Develop own set of values and beliefs.
- Will lose patience with meaningless activity.
- Concerned about body image.
- Find a place in a valued group.
- Search for intimacy.
- Are maturing in abstract thinking. Can consider information and come up with new possibilities.
- Can see self from viewpoint of others
- Search for career possibilities.
- Gaining autonomy. Beginning to accept and enjoy uniqueness.
- Want adult leadership roles. Renegotiate relationships with adults.
- Can initiate and carry out their own tasks without supervision.

The Youth Leader

Dr. Lee Roberson is one of the greatest preachers and leaders who ever lived, he often made the statement "Everything rises or falls on leadership." I believe this principle to be true in all aspects of leadership, in the home, government, business, and most importantly in the church.

If the New Testament Local Church is going to establish an effective youth ministry it must have good biblical leadership with faithful, determined and consecrated leaders. In this chapter we are going to study two aspects, One, we are going to look at the position of the youth leader. Secondly we are going to study the qualities of a good leader.

The Youth Leader's Position

1) The Pastor should choose the Youth Leader.

The pastor should designate a leader over the youth ministry of the church. This person should be carefully chosen. Some pastors spend more time deciding which color to paint his office than he does filling the position of youth leader. If the youth leader chosen does not have experience in working with teenagers, the wise pastor will spend time with the youth leader, sharing his goals and philosophies and will help him put together a plan of action for reaching teenagers and establishing an effective youth ministry.

Another reason it is wise for the pastor to choose the youth leader is so he can relieve him should it become necessary to do so. The youth leader should be an arm of the pastor, as the wise pastor should have his hand on all aspects of the church ministries. The pastor should choose a youth leader that shares his heart for the ministry, and one that is in agreement with him; *"Can two walk together, except they be agreed?"* (Amos 3:3) One who has a burden to reach the teenagers in the area and is willing to work hard at it.

2) The Pastor Leads the Youth Leader.

The pastor must set the guidelines, standards and principles he wishes the youth leader to follow for the teenagers in the youth ministry. No activity should be planned for the teenagers without the approval of the pastor. There are several reasons for this. One to be certain that youth activities do not conflict with scheduled church activities, church events, revival meetings etc.... that the pastor has planned.

Secondly, so that youth activities can be organized to coincide with other church events such as special days, mission conferences, Bible conferences, revivals, and other church wide activities. These will be events the teenagers should be very involved in. Thirdly, so that no activity takes place that the pastor may feel is inappropriate or compromising in the church's standards and convictions.

The pastor should be made aware of any problems that develop in the youth ministry, whether they are behavioral problems, a serious personal problem a teenager may have or other development. I realize some pastors may think the reason they have a youth leader is to deal with the problems, but the significant thing to remember is that the buck stops with the pastor. If there were ever any legal ramifications from any situation that may develop, the pastor would have the brunt of the responsibility. Also the pastor is the overseer of the entire flock, and is wise to be *"diligent to know the state of thy flocks, and look well to thy herds."* (Proverbs 27:23)

3) The Youth Leader must be a Loyal Follower.

The youth leader must be loyal to the pastor. He must never talk negatively of the pastor, especially to the teenagers but should point the teenagers to the authority of the pastor. The youth leader should teach the teenagers to respect the position and person of the pastor.

4) The Youth Leader must be a Good Example.

The character of the youth leader will in many ways come out in the behavior of the teenagers he is leading. It is important that the youth leader have good Christian character with a good moral testimony, good work ethics, and a Christian attitude and respectful to those in authority.

Most importantly he needs a love for Christ, a love for souls and a love for teenagers.

5) The Youth Leader must be Doctrinally Sound.

They should be in agreement with the church's articles of faith, Biblical standards, and should be loyal to the Word of God.

6) The Youth Leader must be a Mature Christian.

I have seen churches put new converts into the position of leadership because the person had an interest in teenagers. This is not wise. You could have a new convert assist the youth leader as an area of ministry for him to serve in the church, but the leader should be a grounded, mature Christian that has proven himself.

If a pastor does not have a qualified person to put into the position of youth leader he would be better off to work with the young people himself and have someone assist him that he can train to become the leader.

7) The Youth Leader Should Have the Full Support of his Spouse.

In my humble opinion it is not wise to have a single young man in the leadership position of the local church youth ministry. I realize there are some fine young men, who love the Lord and want to serve him, but leading teenage girls is not the best area for them to serve in, it creates too many opportunities for problems. Single assistants may be acceptable to help with various youth activities but the primary youth leader should be a happily married man. It is also not wise to have a single woman in the position of leadership. The most successful youth ministries that I have seen have had a married man with a very supportive wife assisting. The wife can be helpful in encouraging the teenage girls and in providing a Christian example for the young ladies to follow.

The husband and wife team must maintain a good marital relationship, especially in front of the teenagers. Setting the example for what a Christian marriage should be like, for many teenagers this will be the only example they may ever see of a Christian marriage.

The husband should lead and the wife should assist him and be his partner in the youth ministry.

8) The Youth Leader must Love God.

This is the number one priority in choosing a youth leader; they must love the Lord, and possess a sincere desire to serve him. The candidate should be seeking an area of service in the church because he wants to serve the Lord, not seeking a name for himself, but seeking people to whom he can serve and help; and willing to do what he is asked to do. He should be a devoted soul-winner and loyal to all the services of the church. There should be evidence in his life of spiritual growth and maturity.

9) The Youth Leader must Love Teenagers.

He does not have to be an expert in youth work; no one is an expert. He does not have to have a college education or have attended seminary. He does not have to understand teenagers, he doesn't even have to know how to work with them; he can learn these things. But he must love them, and he must have compassion for them. A youth leader with genuine love for his Saviour and for teenagers can and will make a difference in the lives of teenagers.

10) The Youth Leader must have a Calling.

The effective youth leader, whether a layman or full time paid staff leader will be one who has a sincere calling from God to work with teenagers. I have heard youth leaders say; "I'm just working with teenagers until I move on to bigger and better things, this is just a stepping stone for me."

Dear friend they are not stepping stones; they are people, people with souls, futures, and we have a responsibility to pass the baton of Christendom on to them. They need leadership, dedicated, loving leadership.

The teen ministry is important and should be led by someone who has a calling for it and has realized its importance.

11) The Youth Leader must be a Soul Winner.

Every youth leader should be burdened for the lost and should be actively pursuing souls for Jesus Christ.

Qualities of a Good Youth Leader

We have looked at some of the qualities of a good leader under the heading of the Youth leader such as, loyalty to leadership and a good Christian example. Now we will look closer at some qualities that make for a good leader whether it is in the position of youth leader, government leader or business leader.

1) A Good Leader is first a good Follower.

I realize that we previously discussed the loyalty of the youth leader to the pastor, but I would like to take it a little further now. Joshua was probably one of the greatest leaders in the Old Testament and the thing that made him a great leader was that he was a loyal follower. A good follower does more than follow the leader with loyalty; he also points other followers to be loyal to leadership. A good youth leader is loyal to the pastor and follows him, but he also encourages the teenagers to be loyal followers of the man of God.

I cannot think of anything more harmful to the youth ministry than for the leadership to undermine the authority of the pastor. This can plant a seed of rebellion in the church that can produce devastating results in the lives of many people, especially the teenagers lives.

2) A Good Leader has a Servant's Heart.

Moses, who led the children of Israel out of bondage and in the wilderness for forty years, was referred to by God, as a servant. A servant holds a very high office in scripture, In Matthew 23:11-12 Jesus said, *"But he that is greatest among you shall be your servant. And whosoever shall exalt himself shall be abased; and he that shall humble himself shall be exalted."*

An effective leader seeks to serve his followers, and a good leader's desire is to meet the needs of his followers. Jesus is the greatest example of a leader-servant, he led the disciples, he taught them, he even scolded them on occasion, but he was also humble enough to wash their feet. In Bible times, feet washing, was a necessary thing to do, as for most people walking was the main mode of transportation. Jesus with his servant's heart met this need for his disciples. An effective leader leads with authority and with the humility of a servant's heart.

3) A Good Leader has Compassion.

Compassion is probably one of the most important characteristics of a good leader, a good leader must have a passion for what he is doing and a compassion for the people he is serving. Webster's dictionary defines compassion as, pity aroused by the distress of others, with the desire to help them. After being in the ministry all these years I have written my own definition of what compassion is and it is as follows. Compassion means I love you where you are and believe you can rise above where you are and I am willing to help you rise from where you are to where you can be.

Teenagers need a leader that will love them in the state they are in, in their family problems, in their peer pressure, when they stumble, when they fall, and even in their rebellion. You do not have to accept bad behavior, but we must accept the one behaving badly. A follower will take correction and will learn from it when he knows that the one correcting him genuinely cares for him.

That teenager who lives in a home of lost parents, who may be on welfare, drugs, alcohol, and living a very immoral life needs some compassion from their leaders. The teenager whose dad is the church pastor also needs a little compassion from their leader. Compassion is sometimes remembering where people came from, while focusing on where they can go.

4) A Good Leader instills Courage

God had to instill courage in Moses to lead the children of Israel. Moses then had to instill courage in the children of Israel time and time again. We see an example of this courage instilling in Exodus 14:13. *"And Moses said unto the people, Fear ye not, stand still, and see the salvation of the Lord, which he will shew to you today: for the Egyptians whom ye have seen today, ye shall see them again no more forever."*

After Moses died, God told Joshua to be courageous three times within nine verses in Joshua chapter one. Jesus instilled courage in the disciples; pastors must instill courage in their people to serve the Lord boldly, to be victorious over sin and to be faithful.

One of the things that made Ronald Reagan a great president was that he instilled confidence and courage in the American people. Reagan personified courage and dignity; and thus the American people were more confident and proud of what they were as a nation.

Confidence and courage in leadership instills confidence and courage in followers. Christian leaders have a responsibility to stand before their followers strong and of good courage and proclaim the truths, promises and commands of God. We have a prayer hearing, Red Sea dividing, gracious, loving, and all-powerful God. The leader must realize that the courage and confidence they express will be transferred to the people he leads. The courage the leader portrays is the security the follower rests in. I am not saying that the follower is to look to the leader as God. I am saying the leader is to look to God with courage and the follower will also look to God with courage. Teenagers will have the courage to live for Christ, to be victorious over sin, to be a witness of the gospel, if leadership instills courage in them by example, edification, and encouragement.

5) A Good Leader has Vision.

I refer again to Proverbs 29:18 which says, *"Where there is no vision, the people perish."* We discussed earlier that vision is a need teenagers and people of all ages have. Vision is a need of followers, but it is a must for leaders.

A good leader has vision for his followers and transfers that vision to his followers, he tells them that he sees them doing great things for God and then encourages them to see themselves doing great things for God. And then encourages them to do great things for God.

On more than one occasion I have heard a parent, youth leader, and even a pastor say to a teenager, "you are never going to amount to anything." If that is what leadership envisions and if that is what leadership tells the follower he envisions them becoming, then that is what the follower will envision and become.

Teenagers today hear enough negative things in society, many of them have a negative vision of themselves and their future, the Christian leadership in their lives must have a higher and brighter vision for them.

6) A Good Leader does not make Provision for Failure.

God told Joshua in Joshua 1:2, *"...now therefore arise, go over this Jordan, thou, and all this people, unto the land which I do give to them, even to the children of Israel."* Joshua then began to prepare the people to cross over. He did not pull out his map and look for an alternative way, and he did not order lumber and draw up plans to build a bridge in case God's plan did not work. Joshua believed God and put God's plan into action. Too much time is wasted looking for alternative ways, new ideas, and modern methods.

My friend God's way will work! When God gives you the guidelines for how to do a thing, you don't need to make any other provisions.

7) A Good Leader seeks Counsel.

Proverbs 11:14 says, *"Where no counsel is, the people fall: but in the multitude of counselors there is safety."* A good leader will learn from studying the ideas, following the proven methods and counsel of the wise and experienced people in their field. A good leader will always seek counsel when making major decisions.

8) A Good Leader Studies.

Someone has wisely said, "Readers are leaders and leaders are readers." Leaders don't just read the Bible a few moments each day; they study it, Second Timothy 2:15 says, *"Study to shew thyself approved unto God, a workman that needeth not to be ashamed, rightly dividing the word of truth."* A good leader studies the principles, methods and biographies of other leaders.

9) A Good Leader Works.

Thomas Edison said, "Opportunity is missed by most people because it is dressed in overalls and looks like work." The opportunity to reach teenagers with the gospel of Jesus Christ in America is tremendous; however that opportunity is dressed in overalls and looks like work. Not only does it look like work—it is work. Booker T. Washington said, "Nothing ever comes to one that is worth having, except as a result of hard work."

In Matthew 9:37-38 Jesus said, *"The harvest truly is plenteous, but the labourers are few; Pray ye therefore the Lord of the harvest, that he will send forth labourers into his harvest."* My friend the harvest of souls among teenagers is plenteous, but laborers are needed and those laborers must labor, they must have the character to work.

The ministry requires work in order to be fruitful. It requires work to visit absentees, it requires work to study for Bible lessons, it requires work to plan and implement activities for teens, and it takes work to make a difference in the lives of people. But the harvest is worth the work.

10) A Good Leader Plans

Jesus said in Luke 14:28, *"For which of you, intending to build a tower, sitteth not down first, and counteth the cost, whether he have sufficient to finish it?"* For anything of magnitude to be accomplished there must be three important things present, One, a dream or idea for what they want to accomplish, Secondly, a willingness to work hard, and Thirdly, a plan. You would not leave the state of

New York to drive to California without setting down and mapping out a plan; you would not begin to build a house without first drawing up a plan of what you want to have as an end result. Good leaders plan, good leaders begin with an end result in mind. In order to have a fruitful youth ministry there must be a plan of action, goals must be set and work must be done.

Plan your activities, soul winning, big days, Bible lessons, and goals carefully. Calculate how many people you will need to help you, how much time you need to invest, how many visits you need to make, and how much money will be needed. See what you want to accomplish, plan what you want to accomplish and then go to work. As the old saying goes, "Plan your work and work your plan."

11) A Good Leader Prays.

Dr. John R. Rice said, "Every failure is a prayer failure." Prayer is the most important part of any leader's life. Our Saviour spent many nights in prayer. The good leader will pray for wisdom for how to conduct his duties. The good leader will pray for compassion to have for his people. The good leader will pray for direction in accomplishing his goals. The good leader prays for the power of God to be on his life. The good leader will pray for his followers by name on a regular basis.

12) A Good Leader helps their Followers Reach a Higher Level of their Potential.

In Deuteronomy 3:28 God told Moses, *"But charge Joshua, and encourage him, and strengthen him: for he shall go over before this people, and he shall cause them to inherit the land which thou shalt see."* God told Moses he would not be permitted to go over Jordan and enter Canaan, but to help Joshua to prepare to lead the children of Israel over into Canaan. God specifically told Moses, *"Charge Joshua, and encourage him, and strengthen him:"* God was instructing Moses to help Joshua reach a higher level of his courage and to give him more responsibility; to prepare him for the task that was before him.

A good leader seeks to help people reach a higher level of their potential. The leader cannot always be with his people and there are going to be times when the follower will have to stand on their own, they will have to be the leader. They will have to cross over their Jordan. They will have to face temptations, obstacles, and situations in which their leader may not be able to help them. So the good leader takes every opportunity to charge (appoint, give command, set in order) encourage and strengthen their followers.

13) Good Leaders Do Not Quit

In his famous speech to a university Winston Churchill said, "Never give up! Never give up! Never give up!" He was without a doubt a man that never gave up. Churchill stayed for the long haul. Institutions, causes, and even ministries that last have leaders that stick to the cause, leaders that stay, and that are faithful to their task. Look at some of the strongest churches we have in America. They are pastored by men who stayed the course, in good times, and bad, during the storms, and the calm, they did not quit when others would have. There is something about longevity, and perseverance that builds greatness.

Dear friend, if you are going to work with teenagers and lead them for the cause of Christ, I implore you, don't give up! I'm not saying that if God calls you into another area of ministry not to go, I'm saying don't give up on the people put into your trust. Don't quit just because a storm comes. The LORD you serve can calm the storms. Don't quit because one has betrayed you. Several betrayed your Saviour, but he did not quit. Don't quit because you think no one is listening, I assure you that if you are proclaiming the truth of Christ with compassion and a prayer in your heart, someone is listening and you will make a difference. I close this chapter with two reasons you should never quit.

1) Someone is Hoping you will Quit.

The drug dealer wants you to quit, the pornography producers want you to quit and Satan wants you to quit. Do not give them the satisfaction!

2) Someone is Hoping you will not Quit.

Your efforts, your concern, and your labor is giving someone hope. The teenager that lives in a drunkard's home is hoping you will not quit. The teenager without a father is hoping you will not quit. The teenager that was contemplating suicide last month is hoping you will not quit. The teenage girl who is going through her pregnancy and has been abandoned by the baby's father and other people in her life is praying that you will not quit.

Ignore those who hope you will quit and live for those who hope you will not quit!

The Purpose of the Youth Ministry

"And, behold, I purpose to build an house unto the name of the Lord my God, as the Lord spake unto David my father, saying, Thy son, whom I will set upon thy throne in thy room, he shall build an house unto my name." I Kings 5:5

Solomon desired to build a house unto the name of the Lord; that was his purpose; that was his specific intention. In order to achieve his desired purpose he had to organize, enlist laborers, and acquire the needed materials.

The purpose of the Temple which Solomon was to build is given to us in II Chronicles 2: 4, *"Behold, I build an house to the name of the Lord my God, to dedicate it to him, and to burn before him sweet incense, and for the continual shewbread, and for the burnt offerings morning and evening, on the sabbaths, and on the new moons, and on the solemn feasts of the Lord our God. This is an ordinance forever to Israel."*

Solomon began to build the Temple with an end result in mind, he had a purpose; he had something he wanted to accomplish for the Lord. If the Local New Testament Church is going to reach teenagers, it must have a purpose for reaching them; it must have an end result in mind. There must be a deliberate and specific intention; it cannot be done properly if it is done haphazardly, without a plan, goals and reason.

Helen Keller Said, "True happiness...is not attained through self-gratification, but through fidelity to a worthy purpose."

Dear friend we have several worthy purposes in reaching teenagers today through the New Testament Church.

1) To fulfill the Great Commission in Bringing Teenagers and their Families to Salvation in Jesus Christ.

We have already discussed several needs teenagers have today, but the greatest need of all is the need of Salvation in Jesus Christ. The most important purpose in having a youth ministry is to reach teenagers with the gospel of Jesus Christ.

Nothing can transform their lives, nothing can help them deal with family problems, help them overcome drugs, or give them victory and peace like them knowing that their sin is forgiven, that God loves them and that they have a home secured in Heaven for eternity. The gospel message should be the center of each and every activity the young people have.

The purpose for each outing, teen meeting, and recreational activity should be to bring lost teenagers to Jesus Christ.

2) To Teach Teenagers the Word of God.

Another important purpose of having a youth ministry is to teach teenagers the Word of God, to give them an opportunity to use their mind.

Nothing will prepare our teens for adulthood like a good dose of Bible preaching and teaching each and every week of their lives. The Word of God should be the focus of the youth ministry; Scripture memorization, topical Bible studies and regular Bible drills will help teens in their spiritual growth. Encourage your teens to read through the book of Proverbs each month. Encourage them to make the Bible the center of their lives. It will help them grow spiritually. No youth ministry should ever have any kind of activity without someone sharing a message from the Bible.

3) To Train Teenagers in Christian Principles and Character.

This is a very important purpose, our young people have been bombarded with the philosophy that character is whatever you think it is, that morals are whatever is right for you, and that what is right for you, may not be right for someone, or everyone else. This is a lie that has deceived many of our teenagers today into destroying their lives. My friend truth is truth, right is right, the Word of God is clear, *"...whatsoever a man soweth, that shall he also reap."* (Galatians 6:7b) For the teenager attending a public school and growing up in a non-Christian home the local church must work very hard to teach them truth, to train them in the way that they should go. For the teenager coming from a good Christian home the local church should reinforce what the parents are trying to accomplish in teaching Christian principles and character in the home and vice versa. Teenagers in the local church should be expected to demonstrate Christian character in their behavior during all activities and youth ministry functions as well as in their own homes. In other words, they should be practicing what they have been learning from us!

4) Spiritual Growth

It has always been my consensus that if a church is growing spiritually it will also be growing numerically. One of the purposes of the New Testament Church is to help God's people grow spiritually, therefore the teenagers in the church should also be growing spiritually. A teenager that got saved last year should now have stronger convictions than one that got saved last week, provided he is involved in a church whose purpose it is to help teenagers grow spiritually. However you may have a teenager that has gotten drunk three times since he got saved and joined your church. But he may have victory now over his drug problem and he is dealing with the heartache of growing up in the home of a drunkard dad. He may not be where you would like him to be in his spiritual life but he is better than he was. Keep in mind that Jesus said, *"And that servant, which knew his lord's will, and prepared not himself, neither did according to his will, shall be beaten with many stripes. But he that knew not, and did commit things worthy of stripes, shall be beaten with few stripes. For unto whomsoever much is given, of him shall be much required: and to whom men have committed much, of him they will ask the more."* Luke 12: 47-48

Some teenagers do not have much of a spiritual home life, you will need to be more patient with them and you may not be able expect the same spiritual growth from them as you do other teens. The important thing to do is to commend effort whenever possible. If you have a very spiritually strong Christian young man in your youth ministry who shares with you that he has surrendered to preach you should commend him for it publicly, let him know that you are proud of him and of his decision. On the other hand if you have a young man in your youth ministry that is a new convert and he shares with you that he has not smoked marijuana in two weeks, commend him publicly as well. Because at his level of spiritual growth, his is just as much an accomplishment as the young man who surrendered to preach and you may find that he will be your next young man to surrender to preach. I am not saying that giving up marijuana is the same as surrendering to preach, the point is that they have both experienced spiritual growth; they are both making progress. And spiritual progress is our purpose!

5) Preparation for Adulthood.

I have often looked at the teen years as training for adulthood. Outside of the family there is no better place to help teenagers prepare for adulthood than involving them in the New Testament Church. I believe the youth ministry of the local church is a vital part of the church; its purpose is not to keep the teenagers separate from the other age groups in the church, but to help get them involved in the growth, ministries, and future of the church. Someday they will be adults; they will have to become responsible for the Great Commission and the preservation of the Bible, and they will become stewards of the gospel.

Therefore the purpose of the youth ministry is to make a place for them to be involved: a place for them to receive training in how to serve in the various ministries of the church, and a place to teach them to respect the leadership of the pastor, and to obey the doctrines of the Bible, and to bring honor to the Lord. It's not all about fun games, and amusement parks; it's about teaching responsibility.

6) To Provide Opportunities for Teenagers to be involved in the Church.

Having a few teenagers attend church services and having a youth ministry with teenagers who are growing spiritually and being involved in the various facets of the church's ministries are two different things. A church with an organized youth ministry will provide a place for the teenagers to be involved. This is not to say that they are to be separate or act separately from the adults, but that they can have a structured means to serve in various activities such as helping out in revival meetings, mission conferences, work days, and other special events. Teenagers are a great workforce in areas of decorating, cleaning, and serving. These things give them an opportunity to serve, learn responsibility and be a part of the work of the church. With supervision they can also be involved in the bus ministry, children's Sunday school, junior church, and of course soul-winning.

7) To Provide Christian Companionship.

I have very fond memories of my teen years growing up in the Emmanuel Baptist Church in Marion, Ohio. We had a wonderful youth ministry under the pastorate of Dr. Charles Hand and a giant of a Christian for a youth leader, Brother Dave Goon, a layman. I developed many friendships in that youth ministry which I still maintain today.

The church youth ministry was my social life, it was my recreation; it was my refuge and the place where I received encouragement and Christian companionship. Teenagers need good wholesome companionship and what better place to get it than with other teens in a Bible based,

Christ centered youth ministry in the local New Testament Church, where the minority is the rebellious crowd, where the odd balls are those who cuss, smoke, and drink. A place where being Christian is normal and where friendship is genuine.

8) To provide recreational and social activities that are clean and wholesome.

I previously mentioned that as a teenager the youth ministry was my social life and my recreational life. It is important to consider that social and recreational activities are important for children, teenagers, and adults. Developing friendships, socializing with other people of the same age helps teenagers emotionally. A structured youth ministry will provide activities that will help teenagers develop good social skills, wholesome relationships, and teach them how to interact with a Christian attitude in recreational events.

9) To Provide a Place of Refuge to Troubled Teens.

It is interesting to me when a pastor or other Christian complains about the troubled teens or the juvenile delinquents in their town, when the same adult that is complaining has done nothing to reach out with the gospel to the teenagers they complain about. They have done nothing to establish an effective youth ministry that could transform the delinquent's life, get the troubled teen off the street, and point teens to Heaven. Many teens hang out on the street, get in trouble with the law, and are involved with the wrong crowd because the right crowd has not provided an alternative for them. It would do us well to remember what my dear friend Mrs. Dolly French often told me when I was young man, "The church is not a sanctuary for saints, it is a hospital for sinners."

An effective youth ministry provides a place of refuge for the hurting teenager, for the teenager with a broken home and a broken spirit. For the teen that is on his way down the wrong road; beginning with telling him about the Lord Jesus Christ and how he can know Christ as his personal Saviour.

10) To Prepare Teens for Leadership in the Church and in Society.

Our young people will not learn about Biblical leadership and citizenship in the public school system or from television programs. It must be taught in the church and in the Christian home. Giving teenagers something to be responsible for will help them build character. Making them think about the decisions they make will help them make right decisions.

And putting them in a properly supervised youth ministry that they have a part in planning activities and events for, meeting the needs of people through Christian service, and sharing the gospel of Christ with others will help them learn leadership skills as well as responsibility.

Just as Solomon had a purpose to build the Temple, let us organize, enlist laborers, and acquire the needed materials for the purpose of building lives that will bring glory and honor to the name of the Lord our God.

Practical Pointers for Youth Leaders

In Nehemiah 4:19 the prophet said, "*The work is great and large,*" And so is the work of the local church youth ministry, it is great and it is large. It is an important work; you are reaching and dealing with people at one of the most crucial ages in their lives. The decisions made during the teen years often affect the rest of a person's life.

In doing the work of a youth leader it is important not to overlook the practical things, the important things about the ministry and the important things about your own spiritual needs and personal life. The following pointers, is like a laundry list dealing with several different aspects of the youth ministry and of working with people; In my view these are some of the most important things for a youth leader to keep in mind.

1) Maintain Your Personal Devotions.

You are dealing with the lives of people, helping them make decisions for their lives, and wrestling against principalities, against powers, against the rulers of the darkness of this world, against the spiritual wickedness is high places.

The young people whom you lead need you to have a fresh relationship with God; they need for you to walk with Him faithfully. And you need the spiritual strength and wisdom that only comes through meditating on the Word of God and prayer. When you share something with your teens from the Bible there should be some evidence in your words and enough compassion in your voice to let them know you have been to the throne of grace on their behalf.

Your enemy is seeking to devour you, he is looking for an opportunity to attack; thus the lamb must walk close to the shepherd.

2) Schedule Personal Family Time.

Do not make all of your family activities youth ministry activities. Plan family outings that you do only with your own children! Take them to the park, shopping, out to eat and to special events. Let them know they are more important to you than anyone in the world. If your children feel like they have to always share you with a gang of teenagers they may become bitter toward you and the teens you are trying to help. Let your family have you to themselves as often as you can.

Take your wife on a weekly date if possible; even if all you can afford to do is go out for a cup of coffee or a soft drink. Your wife and children are your first and most important ministry.

3) Make the Most of your Time.

Ephesians 5:16 says, *"Redeeming the time, because the days are evil."* The youth ministry will keep you busy, many church staff youth leaders have other responsibilities in the church and most volunteer youth leaders have a full time job, so time is a valuable resource, use it wisely. Live by a schedule, plan your teen activities in advance, schedule your study time, visitation time and be certain to schedule time for rest. Have a scheduled time for all of your responsibilities. You will find that you will accomplish more and it will not feel as burdensome for you. As the old saying goes, "Plan your work and work your plan."

4) Involve Your Family in Your Ministry.

Have your family pray with you for the teenagers in your youth ministry. Have your family help you with suggestions in planning activities, take your children with you when you go to visit a teenager, then take your child out for ice cream so you can visit with them for a while.

Have your family help you write notes to teenagers that you are trying to encourage. It is often helpful to a hurting teen if he knows a whole family cares about his needs and problems.

5) Communicate with Your Pastor.

It is wise for the pastor and youth leader to meet once a month, once a week is better if at all possible; to discuss activity plans, review ministry goals, discuss promotions, discuss any potential problems and to share victories. This will help keep the pastor up to date on the progress of the youth ministry as well as give the youth leader the opportunity to learn from his pastor.

If a teenager comes to the youth leader for counsel with a serious problem, i.e. suicidal feelings, says he has been abused, a teenage girl who thinks she is pregnant, or other such situation, the youth leader should notify the pastor immediately. On the other hand when a teenager in the youth ministry has a grand victory in his life, i.e. wins a parent to Christ, kicks a bad habit, or makes any other important decision in his spiritual life, the pastor should be made aware of it so he can encourage the teen with a note or spoken word.

6) Give a Monthly Victory Report.

It is encouraging to the entire church if a victory report is shared with the people once a month from the pulpit. The youth leader could take a few moments in the pulpit during a Sunday morning or evening service and share with the people how many salvation decisions were made in the youth ministry. Report the average attendance for the month in the teen ministry, the number of people who made professions of faith through the teen soul winning efforts! Any major decisions made in the life of an individual teenager could also be shared at this time and you could introduce new teen converts and teen church members to the church by asking them to briefly stand.

This will show the critics that teenagers can be reached for Christ, that they can be productive in the church and that they can live victoriously with a little direction, organization, and encouragement. Giving the victory report also encourages the teenagers to strive for victory and spiritual growth. I realize that some may be critical of this kind of thinking, saying that our motivation should not be for the praise of man.

May I point out that Titus 2:7 says, *"In all things shewing thyself a pattern of good works: in doctrine shewing uncorruptness, gravity, sincerity."* What better pattern could be set for the other teens than to show that the efforts for doing right and serving God is applauded more than what is done on the basketball court with athletic ability? Hebrews 10:25 says, *"Not forsaking the assembling of ourselves together, as the manner of some is; but exhorting one another: and so much the more, as ye see the day approaching."* It is better that we exhort our teenagers in the church service for doing right, than have them exhorted on the street by Satan's crowd for doing wrong.

7) Keep an Open Line of Communication.

If communication breaks down between the youth leader and the young people major problems can begin. To maintain an effective youth ministry of helping teens live victoriously proper communication is very important. Proper communication helps people know that you care about them, it keeps you involved in their lives and in some cases it helps keep some teenagers, "in check".

A) Visit all Absentees as Soon as Possible.

If you have a new convert that misses a youth activity that they said they would be attending you should find out why they did not attend. Most likely someone talked them out of it or they just did not think they would be missed if they were absent. There could be a thousand other reasons, the important thing is that they are a new convert and they need to be discipled; they need encouraged and they need to develop new habits and new friendships with Christians.

B) Get to Know the Parents of Your Teenagers.

The wise youth leader will schedule a time each week to make visits for the youth ministry. Of course this time is going to be used to visit prospects and absentees, but it is also good to make a visit to a faithful teenager's home on occasion just to say hello and to let them know you are thinking of them. Use this opportunity to commend the teenager to his parents and thank them for allowing their teenager to be involved in the teen ministry. This can be a good way of building a rapport with unsaved parents you are trying to win to Christ, and for the parents who faithfully attend the church it shows them that you care about their teenager as well and that you are faithful and sincere in your task.

C) Visit Visitors as Soon as Possible.

Every visitor attending a youth function should be visited before the next scheduled church service. If a personal visit is not possible a phone call inviting them back and possibly scheduling a time to visit them will show your interest in them.

D) Go after the Lamb that has Strayed Away.

I'm thankful that God never gives up on anyone. The teenager who strays away from the Lord, from church and from what is right needs a shepherd that will care enough to go after him, to capture him back from the roaring lion that seeks to devour him. You do not have to hound him; you do not need to go to his home and preach to him. But he does need you to stop by from time to time and let him know you love him that you are concerned for him and that he is welcome back into the fold. Don't give up on them. Expressing that you are genuinely concerned will make a difference.

E) Send Notes to Visitors.

A form letter can easily be made on a computer. The youth leader should send a note to every first time visitor attending a church service or youth activity. Of course in order to do this you will need to get their name and address when they visit!

F) Send Notes to the Faithful.

There is nothing like knowing your efforts are appreciated. An occasional note to those teens who are striving to be faithful in attending the services at church, trying to live for the Lord and do right will be encouraged greatly by receiving a simple note from his youth leader from time to time. It would not be very time consuming to send out three to five such notes each week, depending on the number of teens you have. This is something that the youth leader and his wife could do together.

G) Send Notes to Those who are Struggling.

The young person that has problems at home or is struggling as a new convert with peer pressure or overcoming bad habits will benefit greatly by receiving a note that simply says, "I'm glad you are part of our teen ministry. I am proud of your faithfulness and efforts in serving the Lord. I believe God is doing great things and has a special purpose for your life. I'm praying for you. I am your friend (signature)."

H) Send a Note to the Lamb that has Strayed Away.

As earlier discussed it is important to go after the lamb that strays. One of the ways to go after them is to send an occasional note. Your note may read as follows, "Dear_______, Just wanted you to know that we miss you at church and at the youth activities. We love you and would love to see you this Sunday in church. If there is anything I can do for you, let me know. I'm here for you. I'm praying for you. I am your friend (signature)."

I) Send a Note to Those who have Suffered a Loss.

The teenager whose grandparent has recently passed away, or who may have even lost a parent in death needs to hear from his/her youth leader and needs something they can hold on to. Or whose parents may have separated or divorced could be encouraged and comforted by a thoughtful note from a concerned youth leader.

J) Send a Note to Those who Make an Extra effort in their Spiritual Growth or do Something Without being asked.

Let them know that you have taken notice of their effort and that you are excited about what God is doing in their life. It is usually best if both the husband and the wife sign notes sent to teenagers. It is wise for most notes sent to teenage girls to be from the youth leader's wife, making mention of the youth leader but from and signed by the wife.

8) Discretely Share Disappointments.

When a teenager has let you down for whatever reason, it is not wise to try to humiliate him/her in front of everyone, and in some cases you will only make matters worse. I have always believed it is best to correct in private and commend in public. I realize someone may ask what about making an example of the troublemaker? I believe you can be stern with the troublemaker without being humiliating. Most trouble making teenagers are looking for attention, not to cause trouble, some of your new converts and some from problem homes will not always know the proper way to behave, part of your job is to teach them from the Word of God and by example. Many times you can adjust a trouble-maker's behavior by pulling them aside and telling them you are disappointed in their behavior and that you know they can do better, and then ask them to try harder.

9) Do not try to be a Teenager.

Teenagers are not looking for someone to be like them; they are looking for a leader and security. The youth leader should not try to dress as worldly teens do, he should not try to act as though he is a teenager; these things do not attract teenagers, so act like a mature adult. I am not saying it would be wrong to have fun and cut-up with the young people in a fun loving way. I am saying don't let things get out of hand; do not let your behavior keep you from being their leader.

It is also wise for a youth leader not to pick up on new slang terminology that the teens may use. Most of this kind of thing comes from television or rock musicians. The youth leader should set a good example by using good Christian vocabulary.

10) Do Not Allow Your Teenagers to call You by Your First Name.

Respect should be expressed to authority; there was a time in our society when a young person never addressed an adult by his or her first name. I believe that would be a good thing to return to. It is not wise to allow the teenagers in the youth department to address the youth leader by his first name. The leader is not an equal, he is the leader, he has responsibility, he watches for their souls. Introduce yourself by what you wish to be called. I have always allowed my young people to address me as "Brother Don" this is the way in which I introduce myself to them.

It is helpful if the youth leader's wife addresses the youth leader as the teens should address him when in their presence. And the youth leader should address his wife as, in my case, "Mrs. Debbie", or you may wish to use, "Sister" in place of "Mrs." when in the presence of the teenagers.

11) Teenagers will get Excited about whatever you are Excited about.

I once asked a very successful business man who had a large sales force working for him what the secret to his success was, his reply was this, "People will get excited about whatever you are excited about." There is a lot of truth to that statement, because, the attitude of the follower, is a reflection of the attitude of leadership. If you want the teenagers to get excited about learning the Word of God then leadership must be excited about learning the Word of God. If you want the teenagers to get excited about soul winning, then leadership must be excited about soul winning. May I also add that if you want the church to get excited about reaching teenagers for Christ in your city, leadership must be excited about it, beginning with the pastor!

If you want the teenagers to get excited about being on fire for the Lord and living above the world in victory, then leadership must possess a positive victorious attitude. The average follower will never rise above the spiritual level of his leader.

12) Develop Personal Relationships with your Teenagers.

Learn what your teenagers are interested in, find a common ground on which you can converse with them. Of course we can always talk about the Lord and what they are doing to serve Him. But it is helpful if you can also show an interest in teenagers in other areas. For example, if you have a teenage boy that is a big fan of a particular football team, discuss how his team is doing. If you have a teen that is working on particular project in school, ask them how it is going. If you know that their dad has started a new job, ask how things are going for their dad. If a family member has been ill, ask them about it. If you know that a teenage boy has an interest in cars

(I don't know a teenage boy that does not have an interest in cars), ask them what they think about the new models etc...

Compliment them on little things, like haircuts, new clothes, any effort they make to improve themselves and let them know that you take notice of them as an individual. These things help you build rapport and individual relationships. May I add here that a wise male youth leader will not be too personable when complimenting a young lady and it is best if he does so in the presence of his wife!

13) Be Genuine

Young people are looking for something that is real; they have seen the world try to simulate love in Hollywood movies, in music and on television. Many have tried to find joy in alcohol, drugs, immorality, and have found these things to leave them empty. They are looking for someone that genuinely cares about them; someone that will tell them the truth and that will not compromise on their convictions. As the youth leader you represent your church, your pastor, and more importantly the teenagers you are ministering to, you represent the Lord Jesus Christ.

Be yourself, be genuine in your concern for them; be genuine in your praying, preaching and teaching. Offer them something that cannot be compromised, a dedication that is genuine and unconditional. As the old saying goes, "They do not care how much you know, until they know how much you care."

14) Know Your Adversary.

First Peter 5:8-9 tells us, *"Be sober, be vigilant; because your adversary the devil, as a roaring lion, walketh about, seeking whom he may devour: Whom resist steadfast in the faith, knowing that the same afflictions are accomplished in your brethren that are in the world."* Satan wants to destroy all that you are trying to do to reach teenagers. He wants to discourage you and defeat you anyway that he can. He will attack your teenagers, he will attack your marriage, he will attack your children, he will attack your pastor, he seeks to devour and he wants to stop you. Be on guard, be sober (discreet), be vigilant (watchful), the more ground he gains the more he wants to take. Consider these areas to be sober and vigilant in.

A) Never be Alone with a Teenage girl, and it is not advisable to be alone with a Teenage boy.

Don't trust your flesh and don't trust their flesh or their gossip or the gossip it could create in others. First Thessalonians 5:22 warns us, *"Abstain from all appearance of evil."* And Romans 14:16 says, *"Let not then your good be evil spoken of:"* If you have to talk with a teenager alone, have your wife or other responsible adult present. This will be discussed further in the chapter on counseling teenagers.

B) Never touch a Teenager in any way that could be perceived as inappropriate.

About the most you should ever need to do is shake their hand. Let your wife hug the girls and she should be discreet in doing so. It is very unwise for a male youth leader to develop the habit of hugging any female he is not married to or that is not his mother. You can shake their hand, and you can use both of your hands, to gently and firmly shake their hand, but that should be the limit.

Some teenage girls may be without a father and are looking for male affection; you can provide the attention and affection they need without touching them, by being reliable, expressing concern and love for them. But be on guard about touching them.

Keep watch over your teenagers, Satan wants to destroy their lives, watch for their souls, and guard against the attacks of the enemy.

15) Protect Yourself from Discouragement.

Teenagers can break your heart, you will want to reach all of them, and you will want to help all of them. Some of them will let you take them so far and then they will backslide, they will fall and fall hard. Some of them will make decisions that will alter their lives in a devastating way. There will be times when you will feel like you invested all that you have into a teenager only to have them turn against you or waste all that you have invested. No matter what they do, never stop loving them and never give up on them. I often remind myself of something Dr. Lester Roloff said years ago, "We have enough successes to keep us encouraged and enough failures to keep us humble." Dear Friend, when the discouragements come, we must look to the successes, and keep your focus on the victories and the teenagers that need you and want your help. And most importantly, look unto Jesus, he will give you the strength to move forward. *"Therefore, my beloved brethren, be ye steadfast, unmovable, always abounding in the work of the Lord, forasmuch as ye know that your labour is not in vain in the Lord."* I Corinthians 15:58

Organizing the Youth Ministry

"Let all things be done decently and in order."
I Corinthians 14:40

For a youth ministry to be effective it needs to have several things in place. As we have already discussed it needs to have a leader; it also needs to have a defined purpose and it must have organization, there must be a course of action, procedures to follow that can keep things going smoothly and enable the ministry to be productive and successful. If you study the history of successful ministries and even businesses you will find that the reason for their success was not necessarily genius, but hard work, goals, and a planned course of action. Organization is the key to having a successful local church youth ministry.

1) The Youth Ministry Schedule.

A) The Annual Schedule.

It is wise to have a yearly plan for such things as youth camp, youth conference, special days and promotions within the Sunday school and teen departments. The pastor should share with his leaders his personal plans for scheduled annual church meetings such as mission conferences, revivals, special speaker Sundays, Big days, etc. so the youth ministry schedule can be developed around the church's schedule.

The monthly activities should be outlined in the annual schedule. For example, if you know that you will be attending a youth conference or taking your teens to a church camp in July, you would plan that in your annual schedule so you can begin promoting that activity in April. You may want to schedule a "camp fund raiser" for April and May. Also your summer activities for your teens will be a little different than your winter activities. Having a general plan in advance will help you stay on top of making necessary reservations for various activities that require a lot of preparation.

B) The Monthly Schedule.

The monthly schedule would include your monthly activity and any special church wide events like a revival meeting. Your monthly schedule would keep your weekly activities organized. Each week you promote the upcoming monthly big event, each month you would promote the upcoming annual big event such as youth conference or church revival.

My philosophy is to have one major activity per month for the teen ministry. This activity does not always have to be "entertaining", but its focus should always be evangelistic. There will be much more discussed on this issue under the heading of major monthly activities.

C) The Weekly Schedule.

The weekly schedule is the most intense schedule. I view the weekly schedule in the teen ministry as the vehicle that keeps teens steadily climbing up the mountain, with the monthly schedule bringing them to the mountain top and the annual events give them the view from the mountain top. There are several important weekly functions that the teen ministry can have in place that will produce spiritual growth among the teens and I believe will aid in producing souls saved and added to the church. We will examine them in the following weekly headings.

Before I do so, allow me to make this observation; I believe in big days, I also believe that every Sunday is a big day, every time the Word of God is preached it is a big event in Heaven and on earth. Every weekly activity should be Christ centered and thus promoted, prayed over and carried out to the best of our ability.

2) Weekly Sunday School.

The Sunday school ministry of the church is a vital part of both the church's spiritual growth and the teen ministry's growth. This is a time for Bible study and a time for God's people to be challenged in truth. A focus on Scripture should be made to the teens in the Sunday school time. Some of them we only have for about forty five minutes, the public schools have them all week, the television has them every evening, we must use this weekly Sunday school time wisely with study, preparation of heart and much prayer.

In the Sunday school time be sure and get the name and addresses of every visitor to be followed up later. Make all visitors feel welcomed and important. Promote the teen ministry, upcoming activities and events. The Sunday school teacher should be sure to introduce the youth leader to any teen visitors so he can get acquainted with them before he goes to visit them in a few days. As we already discussed, we visit all visitors ASAP. Every teenage visitor should receive a visit from the Sunday school teacher and the youth leader before the following Sunday.

3) Weekly Teen Meeting.

Some churches title this meeting "Teen Time" or "Afterglow". I think the best time for this weekly meeting is before or following the Sunday evening service. This would be a time of light refreshments, fellowship and a brief but challenging message from the Word of God to the teens. Forty-five minutes to an hour is a sufficient amount of time for this meeting. This can also be a time to give visiting preachers a few moments with the teens, such as missionaries, evangelists and others.

I would never have a guest preacher in that would not speak with my teenagers. If he cannot give a few minutes to my teens, he does not need time in my pulpit and he does not need my love offering. On occasion the pastor can come in and speak to the teens; it is also an encouragement to the teens if the pastor can spend a few minutes in the teen meetings occasionally for fellowship.

The weekly teen meeting also helps get the teens back to church on Sunday night, which helps them grow spiritually and gets them more involved in the church. Some of my fondest memories as a teenager; were attending the weekly Teen Time meeting at Emmanuel Baptist Church in Marion, Ohio, where I had the privilege of hearing many great preachers and missionaries. I established lifelong friendships and God did a work in my heart.

4) Weekly Teen Soul winning.

We will have a whole chapter on the subject of "how to" in teen soul winning. But let me say here that teen soul-winning is one of the most important areas in the church's teen ministry and should be kept on a high level of priority in the weekly schedule of the teen ministry.

5) Weekly Teen Visitation

This should be a time scheduled each week when the youth leader focuses on visiting teenage prospects, absentees and any recent visitors.

6) Choosing a Teen Ministry Name.

This is not something that is absolutely necessary but I believe it can help build a comradeship among the teenagers. The teen ministry name can be voted upon using suggestions made by the youth leader. The teen ministry name also makes the teens feel like they are part of something, everyone wants to be a part of something, and it helps give them purpose.

Some suggested teen ministry names would be Teen Ambassadors, Teen Conquers, and Crusaders for Christ. Use your imagination and that of your teenagers to come up with a name that will be Christ honoring.

7) Choose a Teen Ministry Verse.

Let's say that you decided to call your teen ministry the Teen Ambassadors for Christ. You could then choose Second Corinthians 5:20 as your teen ministry verse, which reads, *"Now then we are ambassadors for Christ,"* An Ambassador is a representative. Choose the verse of your leading and have all the teens memorize the verse, and let it become part of the opening commencements at your activities and teen services to quote the entire verse in unison before prayer.

8) Write a Teen Ministry Mission Statement.

In one sense the ministry verse is a mission statement but it is also a good project for the teenagers, under the supervision of the youth leader to establish their own mission statement. The mission statement would define what the teen ministry wants to accomplish as a group and in their own lives and in reaching the lives of others. I do not want to give a sample mission statement except to say that it should be scripturally based, Christ centered, and should describe well the intentions of the youth ministry.

9) Have a Teen Ministry Brochure.

The ministry brochure should be simple and to the point. A tri-fold style brochure or 3-½ inch leaflet style on card stock works nicely. This size also fits easily in a shirt pocket. The brochure should include the ministry name, purpose and mission statement, the youth leaders name and phone number, the church's name, pastor's name, church location and phone, also list time and days of all youth services. If you go with the tri-fold brochure include the plan of salvation as well.

10) Teenage "Hot Line" Phone Number.

This phone number could be the youth leader's home number or his cell phone. The purpose of this would be for teens to have a number to call if they needed transportation to church or youth activities. Also by referring to the number as the "Hot Line" makes it easier to remember! Having the Hot Line number on your youth ministry brochure, card and other literature that you make available, may encourage a teen to call you in a time of spiritual need; because the "Hot Line" number gives the perception that you are available and able to help in a time of crisis, which of course you are, because you are in the teen ministry.

11) Flyers for Activities

Every event and activity should be a big event! Go all out! Build excitement. Make up some flyers announcing the time, place, and event you are having. Put a brief reminder of the dress code for the activity. Encourage all of your young people to bring visitors to every activity and make every activity evangelistic.

12) Ministry Stationery.

Having ministry stationery adds to the importance and professionalism of the teen ministry. Have the church's name, youth ministry's name, pastor and youth leader's name, mailing address and phone numbers on the stationery. You can also put the youth ministry's theme on the stationery.

13) Ministry News Letter

A simple one-page form letter sent to each teenager in your youth ministry helps in keeping the lines of communication open. In the newsletter you can announce activities, the soul winning schedule and other important events. You can also introduce new converts that have joined the youth ministry and you can share a brief devotional.

14) Define the Rules and Standards.

In organizing the youth ministry one of the first things you will want to do is establish what the rules are. How the young people should behave in the classroom setting, and on activities. Have in writing the dress standards, behavioral guidelines, music standards, items that are not permitted on activities such as walk-mans, alcohol, drugs, and drug paraphernalia, etc. When making your list of rules and standards include the purpose of the youth ministry. Point out that we want to glorify God in all that we do and that we intend to have fun serving the Lord but that we are going to do so in a way that brings honor to Him and not reproach.

15) Monthly Major Activity.

We will not get into a lot of detail here concerning the various types of youth activities to have for your teens. We will be more specific with that in the chapter on activities. However I will encourage you here to schedule one major activity a month. This should be an opportunity for the young people to have some fellowship with other teens, be challenged with a Bible message, and have something to which they can bring lost acquaintances and new converts. These activities should of course be planned months in advance. The better the activity is planned, the better attended and the more enjoyable the activity will be.

16) Annual Youth Camp or Conference.

There are several good church camps and youth conferences around the country to choose from. Camp or youth conference is a great experience for young people. It gives them the opportunity to meet other teens that hold the same convictions and Bible teaching they are being taught in your church. It also gives God the opportunity to get them away from the television, rock music, and other bad influences so he can do a great work in their hearts.

Some Suggestions to Consider in Choosing a Camp.

A) Choose a camp or conference with the same standards that you have in your church, more lenient standards will be confusing as well as compromising.

B) Choose a camp that is of the same doctrine you have. One purpose for going to a camp is so the young people can hear at camp the same thing they heard in the pulpit at their own church.

Suggestions about Preparing for Camp.

A) Make sure everyone can afford to go to the camp or conference. Don't leave anyone out! The teenager who cannot afford to go may be the very one that needs to go the most. If you plan ahead there are several things you can do to help raise money for your teens. For example: Have a car wash, have a cook out at a local grocery store and sell hot dogs and hamburgers off the grille. Have the teens sell candy bars. Other ideas would be to have adults, sponsor a teen to camp. Many senior citizens like to contribute to such causes.

B) Read over any material the camp or conference host sends to you. Know what the dress standards are, know what the special activities are, and know what items need to be brought along. Go over this information with your teens thoroughly. Make sure they understand what is required of them.

C) Pray for your teens specifically for any special spiritual needs they may have weeks before camp. If you have any teens for which you have concerns about their salvation, pray for them accordingly.

When you Return Home from Camp.

A) I recommend that when you return home from youth camp or youth conference that you preach a message to the teens about sticking with any decisions they may have made at camp. For example you may want to preach with a theme like "Now perform the doing of it" to help them further commit to the decisions they made. This would not be a time to portray doubt and tear down all that was accomplished in the meeting, but to build confidence in the decisions they have made and to encourage them in spiritual growth and soul winning.

B) Have a "Camp night" or "Youth conference night". This would be a Sunday evening service shortly after the return home to let the young people share with the church any decisions they made during the meetings. This helps confirm their decisions and challenges the adults to be good examples for the young people as well.

"Camp night" also gives an opportunity to invite lost parents of teens who went to camp to visit the church. Many parents will come to a service that is in honor of their children when they will not come for any other reason. Camp or youth conference should be a major annual event for every local church youth ministry. Begin to promote it several months in advance and make mention of it throughout the year.

17) Conduct an Annual "Teen Revival"

A good time for such a meeting is in the late fall or late winter, after the excitement of camp or conference has sort of, "warn down" a little. Teen revival can help keep the focus (weekly soul winning also helps maintain the focus). There are several ways you could have a Teen Revival. Allow me to make a few suggestions.

A) You could have it on a Monday through Friday or Monday through Wednesday night.

B) You could let any preacher boys you may have in your teen ministry preach a brief message each night of the meeting, maybe let them take five or ten minutes before the key note preacher.

C) The pastor could do the preaching or you could have a guest preacher come in that "specializes" in preaching to teenagers.

D) If you have a young man out of your own church that has gone to a Bible college to prepare for the ministry, he would be a good candidate to preach your teen revival.

E) Pray it down and build it up just like you would any other special meeting. Encourage the entire church to attend. Preaching helps everyone and it will encourage the preacher boys to have the church family there for them as well as the other teens. This should be a major annual event in the youth ministry as well as in the life of the church. We must raise-up another generation of leaders and workers for the harvest.

F) Invite other area churches to bring their teenagers and make them feel welcome.

G) Encourage everyone to bring visitors. You could have a nightly promotion and give an award to the one that brings the most visitors each night.

18) Youth Rallies

I am a believer in area wide youth rallies provided the churches participating are in agreement on major doctrinal issues. It is not wise to get your teenagers involved in a monthly, area wide youth rally in which you do not have a say in the music, Bible version used, and standards followed or, if the music and standards are compromising from what you hold to.

19) Getting Teens Involved in the Youth Ministry.

I am convinced that teenagers are looking for something that they can become a part of. What better thing is there to belong to than a local church youth ministry? I am also convinced that the way to teach our young people to be involved in serving the Lord in the local church is to give them some responsibility in the church youth ministry. The following are some suggestions that I believe can help accomplish that.

A) Appoint a Monthly Secretary.

A young lady should hold this position and the duties would include distributing activity flyers, calling absentee girls, calling girls and reminding them of upcoming activities, helping mail out the youth ministry newsletter, keeping attendance etc.

B) Appoint a Monthly Sergeant at arms.

Duties would include helping with the organizing of activities, calling on absentees, making sure the meeting rooms are in order, and being an assistant to the youth leader.

C) Appoint a Monthly Chaplain

This position would be held by a young man of course, but it would not necessarily have to be a preacher boy. All young men should learn some leadership skills and responsibility. These duties would include reading scripture at the beginning of the youth meetings and activities and leading in prayer. They would not have to bring a full-length Bible lesson or sermon, but at least one time in the month they serve they could bring a brief devotion.

There are several reasons I like the idea of rotating these responsibilities. One, it gets everyone involved and not just a select few. The first choice you might have to be the chaplain might learn from being the Sergeant at arms. And the choice for Sergeant at arms might be challenged to a higher level of his own potential by being made chaplain for a month. Use discretion, but don't leave anyone out.

Being organized is far less stressful than not being organized. Plan ahead and stay on top of what you are doing. Pray, love your young people, preach the truth, and you will reach teens for Christ.

20) Inform and Encourage the Church about the Youth Ministry.

It is good for the entire church to see that the young people are active in the church, that the youth ministry is accomplishing something. One of the best ways to do this is to have the youth leader make announcements about youth activities, teen soul winning, and other youth functions from the pulpit on Sunday morning and Sunday evening. A few moments to do this and to give a report about any special highlights from recent activities, such as teens winning people to Christ, will be an encouragement to the church. This also helps develop a good attitude towards the youth ministry so that when a problem may arise in the youth ministry the church has heard enough good things from the pulpit that a bad incident once in a while does not make anyone panic. Also when a little extra money is needed for a special activity for the young people the church is already aware of the progress being made, the work being done and the lives being changed in the youth ministry, they become a little more willing to help.

Prospects, Where to Begin!

Often when I am in churches or conferences, pastors or concerned laymen will ask me, "How do you start a youth ministry?" Or they will say to me, "We have a lot of teens in our area, but we don't know what to do to reach them." Others have said, "We don't have any teenagers in our church and we don't know how to find any." So I want to answer the question of "Where to begin?" by sharing ideas and principles about finding prospects and reaching out to those prospects. We have already established the fact that someone needs to be the leader in the church youth ministry, and that someone needs to reach out to the teenagers so now we will look at where and how to begin doing that.

1) Begin with the Teenagers you already have.

Schedule a meeting with the teenagers already in your church, even if it is just one or two. A good time to have such a meeting would be on a Sunday night after the service, you could have some refreshments and fellowship. Inform them of your plan as youth leader to begin an effective youth ministry that is going to reach out to the teens in the area with the gospel, provide sound Bible teaching and preaching, and have structured activities that will be recreational, character building, and evangelistic. Share your heart with them and then ask them for their help in finding prospects.

2) The Power of the 3x5 Card.

Give each teenager attending your meeting a 3x5-index card. At the top of the card ask them to write their name and phone number, then ask them to write down the names of three to five teenagers they are aquatinted with that do not attend a church on a regular basis. You do not need to get the prospects addresses at this time that will come later.

The next step you will want to take is to schedule and plan an activity for the following month. The best way to do this is to recommend to your teenagers the activity you would like to schedule. Let's say you want to take them bowling. Ahead of time choose a decent bowling alley where the bar is not out in the open or better yet is non-existent and where rock music is not blaring. The best time to go is on a Saturday afternoon. Set the date and time with your teenagers and encourage them to invite everyone they know. Keep checking with them about how many prospects they think are going to come to the activity.

That week you will need to follow up on your prospect list. Remember I told you that we would get the addresses of the prospects later? Here is how we do that. Call your teenager on the phone and say. "Joe, I have been going over the prospect cards we compiled Sunday night and I see that you have three good prospects on your card. I am calling to ask if you can get your phone book out and give me the addresses of your prospects." Give him time to give you the addresses of his prospects, after you have that information you will ask. "Joe, Mrs. Youth leader and I are going to go out Tuesday evening and make some of these visits, would you be available to go with us? We will stop by the milk shake shoppe on our way home." Schedule the time you will be picking the teenager up for visitation. Make certain the teen has permission from his parents to go with you.

3) Get Prospects from the Adult Sunday School Class.

For this you will use a similar method as you did with the teenagers. Ask the adult to put their name and phone number at the top of the card and then to list three to five teenagers they know, from their neighborhood, who perhaps do not attend church anywhere. Pass out some brochures about the youth ministry to them and ask them to get the brochures into the hands of teenagers they know, especially to the prospects they give you. That week you will call the adults on the phone and ask them if they can get the addresses for you. Be sure and thank them for their help and ask them to pray as you attempt to make contact with the prospects. You do not need to ask them to go out with you and your wife, but if they would like to help you make visits, don't turn them down.

4) Meet with the Sunday school teachers who teach younger children.

Ask if any of them have students with teenage brothers or sisters. Have them write their name and phone number down on a 3x5 card along with the student's name that has teenage brothers or sisters. Again you call the teacher to get the addresses and if possible the teenager prospect's first name.

Preparation for calling on prospects

1) Plan your work and work your plan.

We have established the time you are going to begin, who is going to go with you, and the time you will pick them up. You will want to make as many contacts as possible in the time you have available to you for visitation. Let's say that you have scheduled to pick your visitation partner up at 6:30 p.m., I recommend that the latest you would want to go to someone's home uninvited is 8:30 p.m. So this gives you approximately two hours to make your visits. It would be wise the night before you go to look through your prospect cards with a map of your town. If your visitation partner knows some of the prospects you are planning to visit, begin with those prospects. Using a map of your town plan your visits as close together as possible, this will keep you from driving back and forth across town and will help you use your time more wisely. Make a list of the people you want to visit numbering them in the order you want to visit them.

Transfer each prospect's name and address onto individual prospect cards, this will help in distributing prospects' names to other visitation teams and you can make notes of the visit on the prospect card. The cards are also easily kept in a file box, which you can purchase at any office supply store.

2) Pray

The next and most important thing you want to do is spend time praying about the visitation. Asking the Lord to prepare the hearts of the teenagers and their families you are going to call on, ask the Lord for wisdom in talking with them and ask Him for the courage to speak with them as you should. It is wise to pray about visitation every day, a good youth leader is always looking for teenage prospects that he can win to Christ and get involved in the youth ministry so visitation should be a priority on the youth leader's prayer list.

As you approach the time of visitation you will want to keep an attitude of prayer and take time to think about the people you are going to visit and the importance of what you are doing to further the gospel of Jesus Christ and the Great Commission.

3) Appearance

For visitation you will want to dress neat and appropriately. A suit or sports coat and tie would be fine. A lady should wear a dress or skirt and blouse. People are more comfortable inviting strangers into their home if they are dressed nice. Appropriate dress will also give you a level of confidence and the respect of the people you are visiting. Besides, you are representing Jesus Christ. Be sure that your breath is fresh, and it is wise to keep some breath mints in your pocket or mouthwash in your car. Have your hair combed neatly and put a smile on your face. You are about to do the most important thing in the world; you are going to take the gospel of Jesus Christ to people who may have never heard it before.

4) Important items to take with you.

A) A Pocket Size New Testament

I have always felt that it is wise to carry a pocket size New Testament on visitation or door to door soul-winning instead of a large Bible. A large Bible may be intimidating to some people and they may not invite you into their home if they see you with a Bible in your hand. They know there are a lot of "fruitcakes" out there and unfortunately they might think you are one.

B) A Flashlight.

After dark it becomes difficult to see the addresses on homes, so a flashlight will help you find the numbers better. However, you will want to be careful shining the flashlight at people's homes, do not shine it towards their windows, they might think you are a burglar. A flashlight is also helpful for seeing your way as you walk to the prospect's house. Your wife will appreciate that.

C) Brochures and Flyers

Keep a supply of the youth ministry brochures with you at all times, give one to each prospect you call on and pass them out to teenagers you meet at every available opportunity. Do the same with flyers about upcoming youth activities.

D) Gospel Tracts

Every Christian should carry gospel tracts with them at all times to pass out to people when the opportunity arises. It is good to leave a gospel tract with the people you call on, especially if you do not get the opportunity to share the gospel with them.

E) Blank 3x5 Cards

You never know when someone may give you the name of a prospect or when you may meet a teenager you will want to call on later. 3x5 cards are also good to write prayer requests on or to remind yourself of something important you need to do.

5) Help Other Visitation Teams Prepare.

If you have other couples going out to help you by making separate visits, it is wise to assign them the visits they will be making in the order that will save them the most driving time and help them be more efficient. You could have the other visitation teams meet you at your home or at the church before you go out, give the prospect cards to them and pray with them then go your separate ways. Also be certain that they have adequate brochures, flyers, and gospel tracts and are up to date on scheduled youth activities. It is best if you have taken them on visitation with you two or three times before they go out on their own. This gives them an idea of how things should be done. Having others trained for teen visitation increases your efforts.

How to Call on Prospects

You now have everything you need and you are on your way to call on your prospects, your wife and visitation partner are with you, and you are driving to your first visit. When you go up to the door there is no need to take an arm full of items with you. Just take one or two ministry brochures, a few flyers, and have gospel tracts and your New Testament in your pocket. Too many things in your hands can be intimidating and awkward.

1) Introduce yourself, your partner, tell them the name of the Church you are with and announce your Purpose.

You and your visitation partners walk to the prospect's door and you knock firmly on the door, (I knock even if they have a doorbell; it arouses their curiosity and catches them a little off guard). When someone in the house answers the door introduce yourself and the church you are with, for example. "Good evening, (if you are speaking to a man, extend your hand, shake hands firmly and look him in the eye), my name is Don Woodard, this is my wife Debbie and this young man is Joe French. We are with the youth ministry of Beacon Baptist Church on Sandy River Road. Someone in our church gave us David Smith's name and we wanted to invite him to our upcoming activity (name activity). Does he live here?" Wait for their response, If your prospect is there, ask, "May we visit with him for a moment?" If he is not home, ask, "When would be a good time to find him at home?"

A) If Your Prospect is Not Home.

If your prospect is not home you may wish to take the opportunity to find out if the family has a church affiliation and build rapport, so you can share the gospel with them. This opportunity may be opened to you, especially if they are not hesitant to invite you into their home. (Read Chapter on soul winning) When you leave, be sure to give them a ministry brochure, activity flyer and gospel tract, encouraging the family to have the teenage prospect call you and ask them if they would mind if you gave the prospect a call later to invite him to the activity over the phone.

Thank them for their time and courtesy; don't over stay your welcome, leave yourself an opportunity to return to visit your prospect and to witness to them again if they are not saved. You could say something to this effect; "We appreciate your time and courtesy, let David know we came by to invite him to the activity and that we will try to see him another time. You folks enjoy your evening."

When you get to your car write the parents names on the prospect's card and any other pertinent information, such as, if you lead anyone in the home to Christ, or if it would be good for the pastor to visit the parents as potential prospects for church or to witness to them again. It may be a situation of a single mother that might be easily won to the Lord, or would be encouraged to visit the church if a couple of ladies went by for a visit at another time.

B) If your prospect is home.

If your prospect is home ask whoever has greeted you at the door if you can speak with them. Of course if your prospect greeted you at the door you would have a similar introduction. When you begin to speak with your prospect, use the same introduction you used at the door, i.e. introduce yourself, your partner; tell them the name of the church you are with and announce your purpose. Then extend your hand, look them in the eye, and tell them it is your pleasure to meet them. Your introduction may go something like this, "Hello David, my name is Brother Don Woodard, and it is a pleasure to meet you. This is my wife Debbie and this young man is Joe French. We are with the youth ministry of Beacon Baptist Church on Sandy River Road and we came by to meet you and tell you about a special youth activity we have coming up on (give date and time). Do you have a few minutes?" Your prospect may know Joe from school or it could be Joe's prospect so they may be well acquainted, if so it usually makes the introduction and rapport building go smoother. Hopefully by this time you will be invited into the home, if not, ask, "May we come in for a moment." If the prospect's parents are not home it is not wise to go inside. If the teenage prospect's parents are not home but the prospect invites you into the house, you should tell them, "We can't stay, we just came by to meet you and to invite you to the activity." And continue your conversation at the door. If the prospect's parents are home but the prospect displays resistance about you entering the home, there could be many reasons they don't invite you in, they may have company, they may have their pajamas on, you, may have interrupted a meal or other activity. Or they may just feel uncomfortable inviting strangers into their home. Remain at the door and continue your conversation and build rapport, try to make them feel at ease. Telling them you cannot stay long or that you have other visits to make will help them relax and not feel intimidated. Your purpose is not to be invited into their home, but for them to invite Jesus Christ into their life and to become involved in your church's youth ministry. Be patient and work with them.

2) Build Rapport

After you have made your introductions and pleasantries, take a moment to build rapport or to find some common ground. If your prospect is acquainted with your visitation partner, you could use that to establish rapport with a conversation such as, "David, how long have you and Joe known each other?" Give your prospect a moment to respond. "So you two fellows played on the same soccer team last season, did your team do well?" After David responds, you continue the conversation your objective is to make your prospect feel comfortable talking to you and to build a rapport. "David, do you go by David or Dave?" Wait for response and address him by the name he prefers. "Dave, are you planning to play soccer next season too?" The point I want to make is to take a few moments find some common ground, and make your prospect feel comfortable talking with you. If your prospect does not know your visitation partner, ask what school he goes to, what grade he is in, what subjects he likes, if he is in sports etc.... Of course the questions you would ask a teenage girl would be a little different, and with a girl you may have your wife ask some rapport building questions.

3) Present your Purpose

You have found some common ground, and your prospect is comfortable with talking to you, now present your purpose in being there. "Dave, as I mentioned to you earlier, we came by to invite you to our upcoming youth activity. We are organizing a ministry to teenagers that will provide them with some recreational activities and give them a place to enjoy the company of other teens. We usually have one special activity each month and weekly activities at the church, would you be our guest at (name upcoming activity and time) our bowling-pizza party on Saturday the 15th?" Wait for a response, if he says he will definitely attend, say, "That's great, we look forward to it, we will meet at the church at 1:00 p.m. do you have transportation?" Make any necessary arrangements to get your prospect to the activity. Make sure you have his phone number so you can follow up with him.

If for whatever reason he is not certain he can attend, let him know you will check back with him and that he can call you when he knows for sure. The next step you will want to take is to invite your prospect to Church Sunday morning; "Dave as I mentioned we also have weekly activities, would you be available to be our guest this Sunday at our teen Sunday school meeting? We can make arrangements for transportation." This prospect may attend church somewhere on Sunday mornings, at this point your purpose in not to take him out of his church, but to win him to Christ and get him involved in your church youth ministry. I would rather proselyte them if they attend a church that does not preach the truth than let them go to Hell, but my priority is to win them to Christ. So I would take the opportunity to share the gospel with him.

When I pastored in Ohio we had several teenagers that attended our Wednesday night Bible Club that went to church with grandma at the "Church of nothing happening here" on Sunday morning. But they were growing spiritually because of our Wednesday night ministry, they were saved and some of them began attending our Sunday morning services after we worked with them a while.

4) Get Acquainted with their Parents

If your prospect agrees to attend the activity or Sunday morning service, be sure to clear it with their parents. Inform the parents of the time of arrival for transportation, what will be taking place at the activity etc.... Let them know you will be attending the activity, give them a tract and a youth ministry flyer, point out the church's address and phone number, so they will know where their teenager is and who he is with. Thank the parents for their time and for permitting their teenager to attend the upcoming activity. A lot of parents, even lost parents are looking for something that will keep their teens active and out of trouble. Some are looking for a positive influence for their teenager, and the evening you stop by to invite their teenager into your youth ministry may just be an answer to their prayers.

5) Follow Up

If you have a commitment for the activity and for Sunday morning, and won them to Christ, you have made a good visit, however, a commitment does not guarantee a show; you will need to follow up, make transportation arrangements, and pray. One visit is not enough, follow up on everyone. If they do not keep their commitment and attend the activity, go back and invite them again, show a genuine interest in them, as long as they show an interest, you show an interest. If they stop showing an interest, you continue to show an interest. If they made a commitment to attend Sunday school, give them a call on Saturday to remind them, or if possible, stop by their house and remind them. Be enthusiastic; let them know that you are excited about them coming, and that you are excited about the teen meeting. Tell them there will be other teenagers there they will probably know, remind them that your phone number is on the brochure you gave them and that thcy can call you if they need anything.

6) Follow up Phone Call

Your follow up call may be something like this, "Hello Dave this is Brother Don, I'm just calling to let you know my wife and I are excited about you coming to the teen meeting tomorrow, Joe and I will be by to pick you up at 9:30." Notice I did not ask him if he is still planning to come to the teen meeting, I enthusiastically reminded him that he is coming to the teen meeting, I reminded him that I will be picking him up. If he has had a change of mind, it will be difficult for him to back out since I did not leave him an open door to do so.

7) Follow up Letter.

Using your youth ministry stationery write a simple note to let your prospect know that you appreciate their time and that you are looking forward to them attending the teen meeting and reminding them of the time place and transportation arrangements. If you are sending a letter to a teenage girl it is best if the letter is from the youth leader and his wife, using plural pronouns and signing the letter together. Teenagers love to get mail, and receiving one from someone they just met will make them feel important. Such a letter would be similar to this. "Dear Dave, It was a pleasure for my wife and I to meet you Tuesday night and to visit with you if only briefly. I am looking forward to having you in our teen meeting this week. As we discussed, Joe and I will be by to pick you up at 9:30. We are excited about you becoming part of Teen Ambassadors. I know you will enjoy the activities and getting to spend time with the other teens. We have some exciting things planned for the coming months that I know you will want to be part of. See you at the teen meeting. I am your friend, Brother Don."

Not every prospect you visit will attend the youth meeting and some of the prospects you call on will not even give you an opportunity to share your purpose for the visit. Don't be discouraged and don't give up on any of them, love them all. There are a lot of teenagers out there that are lonely and looking for something they can be involved in. You have the greatest thing in the world; you have Jesus Christ, a local New Testament Church and a structured youth ministry with a desire to meet the needs of teens. Keep prospecting, there are some pearls, gold nuggets, and diamonds out there and if you stay at it you will find them!

The Electronic Social Network Age

We certainly live in the generation of communication and information. It seems that everyone has a cell phone and several other electronic devices. Many of our senior citizens have discovered the Internet and use it for a variety of purposes from keeping up with grandchildren to taking on-line college courses. There is no question that with our modern electronic social network age there are dangers, and we have all heard tragic stories of people who have gotten into trouble for using these modern marvels unwisely.

Like so many other inventions over the centuries, the electronic devices at our disposal can be used for both good and bad. The internet by itself is neither, good nor evil. But it can certainly be used for both. The internet is currently being used to promote the gospel of Jesus Christ, to train ministry students and to be a tremendous resource of research and study. But it is also used to promote the message of hate, to train terrorists, and to promote some very wicked behavior.

Therefore in implementing electronic communications in your youth ministry, it is important to stress to your young people the positive uses and to warn them of the dangers of inappropriate uses. These tools are not going to go away, but in many ways are going to become more refined. If we do not use these resources for God's glory, the world is certainly going to take advantage in more ways than one.

Due to my limited knowledge of some of the more recent communication devices and programs available today, I sought the advice of my missionary friend, Harry Peart. The following are some ideas he and I discussed that might be useful.

The most popular forms of electronic social communications available are instant messaging, texting, VOIP, e-mail and social networks. These can be used in a variety of ways to communicate with your teenagers for a variety of purposes, to give a sense of continuity in your youth ministry, and to get a message out in unparalleled speed.

1) A Daily Devotional

A Bible verse with a Devotional message that ties into an upcoming lesson could be sent via e-mail or texting to your teens each morning. You could write your own or sign-up for one from a reputable source.

2) Upcoming Studies

An e-mail with a daily question could prompt study for the lesson that week. Also trivia questions for ongoing class competition can encourage enthusiasm. Sending out a quote that goes along with a particular study can go a long way in enhancing that study.

3) Get the WORD out!

"For the WORD of God is quick, and powerful, and sharper than any two edged sword, piercing even to

the dividing asunder of soul and spirit, and of the joints and marrow, and is a discerner of the thoughts and intents of the heart." (Hebrews 4:12) Occasionally texting or e-mailing an appropriate Bible verse or passage can be a great service to them. The Holy Spirit uses the Word of God to speak to our hearts and sending a verse of Scripture to a discouraged or straying teen can make a positive impact. Also sending Scripture to the entire group and having them all meditating on the same passage will encourage unity.

4) Electronic Prayer Chain:

Urgent prayer requests could be sent out to your teens. This would help them in praying for each other in taking needs to the LORD in prayer.

5) Personal Messages of Encouragement:

Occasionally you may wish to send a note to your teenagers and let them know you are thinking of them. A message can be sent to the group or to individuals who may need extra encouragement. A note of encouragement to the teenager who is facing a big test, or has a family challenge or other discouragement in their life can make all the difference. A simple "my wife and I prayed for you this morning" can mean the world to a teenager who needs encouragement from someone who cares for them. We have a Deaf teenager in our church and he and I communicate often through texting. It is a blessing to be able to keep in contact with him in this manner and I believe it is a blessing to both of us.

6) Activity Reminders:

Electronic communications is an excellent resource to keep in touch with your teenagers regarding activities. The beauty of this is that you can send out an electronic message about an activity that they can in turn forward to their friends.

7) Electronic Visitation:

If one of your teenagers misses a service or activity, you can quickly e-mail or text them to ask if they are all right and find out why they are absent. If you have a visitor and you get their cell phone number or e-mail address, you can send them an electronic thank-you for visiting message.

8) Electronic Invitation:

Using electronic communications you can invite your teenagers to meet you at the local ice cream Shoppe after the Sunday night Church service, after Teen Soul winning, or on Saturday afternoon just for a time of fellowship.

Precautions to Take:

1) Have a Safety Net:

I would suggest that you keep a hard copy of all messages sent and received from teenagers. Also include the pastor in all communications. Almost anything said today can be taken out of context. A wise youth director will guard himself from the easily misunderstood communications. For example when sending a group email, send the pastor a carbon copy. Other ways of accountability may seem too burdensome, but there have been many situations turned bad because of misconstrued intentions. Be on guard!!!

2) Never use Electronic Communications for gossiping:

Don't ever gossip! Humiliating or to embarrass a teenager is never acceptable. What is thought to be a joke to some can be an insult and hurtful to the one on the receiving end.

3) Do not talk about Personal Matters,

your own or anyone else's! What you send can quickly be forwarded literally around the world in a matter of seconds.

4) Don't be Negative:

And don't complain, only use the resource of electronic communications to edify! If you send out jokes, be very selective, what is funny to you may be offensive to others, so guard your testimony!

5) Don't make Electronic Communication a Requirement.

Not everyone's parents can afford a cell phone and some folks don't like them. Some teenagers may be banned by their parents from using the internet because of inappropriate behavior. Be mindful and understanding of these things and make a way for these teens to stay in the loop.

Youth Activities

One of the most important things to keep in mind with having activities for teenagers is that you must keep them busy. It is not good for them to have a lot of idle time during activities. They will get bored and if unsupervised they will sometimes begin conversations that are "inappropriate". The key is to plan your activity well, plan every moment of the activity. Have some songs selected for them to sing, games to play, there are many games young people can play while traveling on a bus etc...

Every activity should be evangelistic, make an opportunity to share the gospel, you may have a lost teenager present. Always share a Bible message. You do not have to preach for an hour at every activity, but something should always be shared from the Word of God. Our primary objective is to honor Jesus Christ.

We have already discussed some activity ideas such as, camp, youth conference, teen revival, and weekly teen soul winning in organizing the youth ministry. But how do we come up with ideas for teen activities?

Finding Activity Ideas

One of the easiest ways to find activity ideas is to ask your teenagers what they would like to do. However there is an organized way to do this that will avoid lengthy discussions and arguments. Using the trusty 3X5 card, take a survey. In your weekly teen meeting, give each teen a card and ask them to write down three activity ideas they would like to do in the future. Let them know it is all right to list activities that will cost money but that you also need ideas that would be inexpensive or free.

If you have some new converts in your youth ministry you may get suggestions like; go to a rock concert, or have a dance, etc. You can disregard these ideas and take an opportunity to teach on those things in a future Bible study. But over all you will get some reasonable ideas from which you can plan some major monthly activities.

Youth Activity and Special Event Ideas

The following are some activity ideas that vary from fun to fancy. May I say again go all out on your activities and make them special for your young people.

1) Picnic

This is a great spring, summer, and fall activity and usually inexpensive. Everyone can bring a covered dish, some soft drinks, and a pack of hot dogs or hamburgers. This is also a good activity for inviting visitors to because everyone loves a picnic. You can play some simple games like Frisbee, softball, three- legged race etc. You can have your picnic at the church, at a local park or at a church member's home.

2) Bowling

This is always popular with teens and can usually be scheduled for a Saturday afternoon. Make arrangements with the bowling alley in advance, ask if you can reserve the lanes furthest from the bar if they have one, or try to find a bowling alley that does not serve alcohol.

3) Visit an Historical Monument.

Do some research ahead of time about the person or historic event it represents! For example if you were going to visit Mount Vernon, (the home of President George Washington) you would want to tell your young people about his Christian faith, that he was a student of the Bible. George Washington was a man of dedicated prayer, spending every evening in what he referred to as his *private religious worship*. This was a time in which he got alone with God for Bible reading and fervent prayer.

4) Attend a Revival Meeting.

This is a great activity; take your teens to hear a preacher who may be holding a meeting in a church that is within driving distance. I remember as a teenager going on such an activity to hear Dr. Lee Roberson, who was preaching at a church about an hour away from us.

5) Project Activity.

The term "project activity" sounds a little more enticing than "work activity" but it is the same thing. Choose a project at the church that the teens could do with a little supervision. For example, they could sweep the parking lot, paint a Sunday school classroom, plant flowers, trim hedges, and clean out a storage room. It is their church too, they can learn to help take care of it and serve the Lord in doing so. This kind of activity also helps keep a good attitude among the adults towards the teens. This activity should be well supervised and planned. Provide a meal for your workers or have them bring a packed lunch, have devotions following the meal.

6) Decorate for Revival, Mission Conference or other Special Event.

The young people are good for passing out handbills for special meetings, hanging banners around the church, decorating Sunday school classrooms etc.

7) Parents Banquet.

This is a wonderful activity that gives you the opportunity to get some of the un-churched parents to visit the church. This is a banquet the teenagers put on for their parents, sort of an appreciation banquet. It is important that this activity be organized well and promoted well.

Between mother's day and fathers day is a good time to schedule this event. Saturday evening is a good time to have it, but the best time is to schedule it for Sunday afternoon around 4:30 PM. The banquet can go up until church time, and the parents can be encouraged to stay for the evening service. Be sure to have "stand in parents". No matter what you do, not all of the parents will attend. Some may have jobs that hinder them but others just will not attend because it is a church activity. You should know your young people well enough to know which parents may not attend and have godly Christians "stand in", in advance. Have each Sunday school teacher, bus captain, and youth worker invite the parents. This should be a big event, and a tremendous opportunity to reach the parents with the gospel. The message given in the banquet should include commending the parents for having their young people involved in church. Go all out, make it first class, and let the parents know that they are appreciated. Share the Gospel. A poem about being a parent would make a nice gift for each young person to give to his or her parents.

8) Thanksgiving Banquet.

This is a good banquet for the teenagers to give to the senior citizens in the church. This can be given on a Sunday afternoon in November. The teens can decorate the fellowship hall, prepare the meal, organize the event and provide special music. It is helpful for the senior citizens in the church to see that the teenagers have some character and are willing to serve and show appreciation. Keep in mind that these are the folks who often give sacrificially to help the various ministries of the church including the teen ministry.

9) Valentine Banquet

This is another special time for the teenagers. However I do not think it is wise to promote every one needing a “date”. We will discuss dating later in the chapter on Boy friend and Girl friend relationships. You could make it an, “I love Jesus banquet”. The teens could host this banquet for the widows in the church or just make it a special time for thinking of the Lord and the Love he has for us.

10) Soul Winning Blitz

Take the teenagers out to a designated area on a Saturday afternoon to go soul winning. Have plenty of adult supervision, equip them with gospel tracts and encourage them to share the gospel with as many people as they can. Afterwards meet back at the church for food, fellowship and testimony time about the blitz. Be sure to get the names and addresses of those who make professions of faith for follow up purposes.

11) Gospel Tract Blitz

This is an idea activity for those who are not yet experienced soul winners. Equip your teens with gospel tracts and go to a heavily populated area. All the teens have to do is hand out a gospel tract and say, “May I give you a gift?” or “This will tell you how to get to Heaven.”

Try to keep a record of the approximate number of tracts passed out in this event. Be sure the tract has your church’s name, address and phone number on it. Afterwards meet back at the church or at a local restaurant for some food and fellowship.

12) Harvest Party or Hobo Party

This is a good activity to have in place of Halloween. Everyone can dress up like Hobo’s and you can make a big pot of stew. Games like apple bobbing can be played. Give an award to the best boy and girl Hobo outfit.

13) Game Night

This is a good winter activity. Gather up several board games for the young people to play. You can have competition on certain games to get a champion. You can have a boy and girl champion. Have 1st, 2nd, and 3rd place winners. It can be a game marathon. Serve refreshments, pizza, tacos, or hot dogs and soda always do the job.

14) We Love Missionaries.

This is a great activity on the Saturday of the Missions conference. Invite the missionaries and their families to a game day at the church. Like with game night, you can play board games or picnic type games. Have special gifts for the children of the missionaries that are present. Let it be a time of fun and relaxation for the missionaries and their children. Provide a meal and have time for a Bible message. Do not ask a missionary to speak, use this time to bring a message from the Bible to show your appreciation to the missionary. This time can also be used to encourage your teens to missions. Missionaries are servants of the Lord and should be honored as such.

15) Olympics

This is a fun summer activity for teens. Organize some fun outside games that could be done in Olympic fashion. Use as many team games as possible. Not everyone is an athlete and some may be intimidated by competition.

16) Hiking Trip.

This is a great activity for teens; they can use up some of that energy, get some exercise, and enjoy the fellowship. A packed lunch would be in order, plan ahead by locating a good hiking trail in a nice park or scenic area.

17) The "All Niter" or "Late Niter".

This is the infamous big activity that always draws a crowd. The all night activity usually includes a late night trip to the bowling alley, the Y.M.C.A for basketball, volleyball, Ping-Pong, and swimming. Pizza is always popular. Sometime in the night there is a movie and always there should be a time for preaching and a gospel invitation. If you do not yet have a large youth ministry you may want to include other churches in this event. It is best to make this annual event in the winter months. It usually does draw a big crowd and is an excellent means of getting prospects and reaching teens for Christ. Plan in advance, have plenty of chaperones, and an organized schedule with little if any "down time".

18) Sunday Afternoon Program.

Having a Sunday afternoon program is a wonderful way of strengthening your teen ministry and increasing your teen attendance for the Sunday night service. It is something that you could develop into a monthly, bi-weekly or weekly activity. Of course a Sunday afternoon program would need to be well organized and well supervised. You could begin with a meal, then some time of recreation followed by a time of Bible training and preaching. This time could be used to give some of your preacher boys an opportunity to preach.

The Sunday afternoon could also be used as a time to take the teenagers soul winning, or down town to pass out tracts. You could separate the boys and the girls and teach on dating issues, and other topics that may be more helpful if taught separately. The Sunday afternoon program is a wonderful means of helping the bus teenager grow spiritually and get more involved in the church youth ministry.

19) Christian Service Activity

This is an activity in which the teenagers help someone with a special need. For example the young men can trim the hedges and mow the lawn of a shut-in while the girls prepare a special meal, plant flowers in the yard, tidy up the house and everyone can visit with the shut–in for a time of fellowship. Many of our shut-ins, widows and widowers are lonely, let us not forget them. Food can be prepared and taken to widows on a Saturday evening.

Find someone with a need and fill the need. Invite the senior citizens to the church for a cook out on a Saturday afternoon and while they are eating have the teenage boys wash their cars for them. That is what the Christian life is about, serving Christ through serving others.

"Pure religion and undefiled before God and the Father is this, To visit the fatherless and widows in their affliction, and to keep himself unspotted from the world." James 1:27

20) Amusement Park.

This is the big summer activity that always draws a crowd of young people. Be sure to remind your teens of the dress code. Invite plenty of visitors of which you will want to follow up on. Reserve a place at the amusement park where you can have a time for the Bible message and gospel invitation. Have plenty of chaperones.

21) Miniature Golf Outing.

22) Attend a Sporting Event.

23) Canoeing

24) Fishing on a Chartered Boat or off the Riverbank.

25) Make parent appreciation baskets. Have your teens make baskets with their parents favorite treats in them include an appreciation card.

26) Make appreciation baskets to be sent to missionaries or evangelists.

27) Make an Appreciation Basket for the Pastor and his family to be presented to him in the Sunday evening service.

28) Take a Trip to The Zoo.

29) Have a homemade ice cream party and invite the pastor, church staff, and their families to be the guests of honor.

30) Take a Scenic Tour of the Christmas Lights in Your City.

31) Visit a Car Show.

These are a few ideas you can begin with. Keep your teens involved, give them good clean things to do, and teach them to serve the Lord, love them and your youth ministry will grow.

Teen Prayer Band

The Purpose of the Teen Prayer Band:

-To teach teenagers about prayer; Jesus taught his disciples how to pray.

-To unite teenagers through prayer in the local New Testament Church.

-To involve teens in praying for Revival in America, for their families, their pastor, their church, and each other.

-To give God the opportunity to show our young people that He still answers prayer.

-To invite God to work in the lives of our teenagers.

What To Have The Teens Pray For:

-Pray for the Lost.

-The first step would be to share prayer requests, people who are sick, family needs or other personal needs, such as lost family members and acquaintances.

-Pray earnestly for revival in your church and community.

-Pray for the pastor.

-Pray for their parents and families.

-Pray for special needs in the church.

-Pray for any and all special needs and situations that

affect the lives of the young people, whether it is one of them or all of them.

What You Will Need:

-An appropriate place to meet, a Sunday school class room is a good place.

-We suggest that the boys and girls meet in separate places to pray.

-Have a group prayer journal to record answered prayer, the leader could begin each session by reviewing the past weeks prayer requests that were answered.

How to Get Started:

-Leadership is crucial, so we suggest that the youth director and his wife lead the prayer meeting. We also encourage the pastor and his wife to attend the teen prayer band whenever their schedule permits. The pastor may want to lead the Teen Prayer Band, or at least attend on a monthly basis.

-Choose a date to start.

-Choose a weekly time to conduct the teen prayer band and STICK TO IT! We suggest Sunday evening before the service or Wednesday evening during "Prayer Meeting" time.

-Opinions vary on how to conduct a public prayer meeting; you may wish to break up into twos, or you may wish to call on four or five different people to pray aloud. Some may prefer to just have everyone pray silently or aloud. The important thing is that teenagers get a grasp of the truth that prayer works and that teenagers can, and should have a prayer life.

Begin each prayer meeting with scripture reading on prayer, encourage the teenagers that God loves us, He hears and answers prayer.

-We suggest that you teach the teenagers to kneel down when they pray, no one in the Bible was ever sitting down when they prayed. We are praying to God, the one who loves us more than any other, kneeling shows reverence to Him and humility on our part.

-Allow 25 to 30 minutes for the prayer time. Five minutes to read scripture and give an answered prayer report. Five minutes to take prayer requests and fifteen to twenty minutes to pray.

What to Expect:

-More spiritual teenagers.

-More people saved.

-A growing teen ministry.

-God's blessing!

-Revival!

Time is short so let's get started, and let's teach our Teens to Pray!

"And it came to pass, that, as he was praying in a certain place, when he ceased, one of his disciples said unto him, Lord, teach us to pray," Luke 11:1

"Ask, and it shall be given you; seek, and ye shall find; knock, and it shall be opened unto you:" Matthew 7:7

"Again I say unto you, That if two of you shall agree on earth as touching any thing that they shall ask, it shall be done for them of my Father which is in Heaven."

Matthew 18:19

"And all things, whatsoever ye shall ask in prayer, believing, ye shall receive." Matthew 21:22

"And this is the confidence that we have in him, that, if we ask any thing according to his will, he heareth us: and if we know that he hear us, whatsoever we ask, we know that we have the petitions that we desired of him."

I John 5:14 -15

"If prayer is good, then more prayer is better."

—Dr. John R. Rice

"Until we have prayed, we have done nothing."
—Dr. Tom Williams

"Every great move of God has been started by teenagers."

—Charles G. Finney

"In the 1960's one generation made a difference in America for rebellion. I believe this generation can make a difference now for the future of America."

---Dr. Don Woodard

Financing the Church Youth Ministry

Having a productive teen ministry is exciting and it can and will produce fruitful lives. However it does take money; I have seen too many churches not want to reach out to teenagers because they say they cannot afford to. Dear friend, may I say that our teenagers cannot afford for us to not reach out to them! I am glad the Saviour did not say he could not afford to go to the cross! I have found that churches can usually afford what they want. If they want the bus ministry they will find a way to afford it. If they want a productive youth ministry they will find a way to afford it. Well, enough of my preaching. I surveyed twelve pastors and interviewed several others about the youth ministries in their churches. One of the topics I asked was How do you finance your youth ministry. The following are some accumulated ideas that were shared with me.

1) Charge enough for the cost of specific activities to cover most of the expense.

The church supplements the unpaid amount from the general fund. When the event is ministry related (soul winning, bus ministry etc.) the church pays.

2) Encourage the parents and others in the church to give to the "youth fund" which is used to pay for special youth activities and to buy food for special youth events.

3) Have teens support their own ministry with fundraisers such as car washes, candy sales etc.

4) Take special free will offerings for special youth events that may cost a little more than some teens may be able to pay.

Raise money through the free will offering for some projects until the need is met.
The Church supplements from the general fund.

5) Put one percent of church offerings into the youth fund.

This would be used to purchase candy and some promotional items for the bus ministry and the youth ministry. This fund and having teen's help with a few dollars for big events usually meets the needs.

6) Teens raise all their money for camp with car washes, candy sales etc.

This helps them appreciate camp more because it is something they have worked for. Most of the church people will get their car washed at the car washing activity to help out.

7) Have an annual cookout in a local grocery store parking lot.

Make up signs that say, "Send us to the youth conference". The grocery store will gladly sell you all the hot dogs and hamburgers you need. A soft drink distributor will set up a booth for you with fountain drinks and you pay for what you sell. The drink sales are very profitable. The teens can work the grille and cola stand. The town folks like to see young people earning their own way. You can also hand out a gospel tract and church literature with each sale at the booth.

8) Have a set amount of money go into the youth budget each week from the offering received.

$25.00-$50.00 a week can go a long way if activities are planned and budgeted carefully. Generally money can stretch a long way for activities if they are planned, organized and budgeted for in advance. The fund raising events such as car washes are youth activities in themselves. Many fast food restaurants will permit churches to have a car wash using their water. It helps bring in customers on a Saturday afternoon for their business. The teens can usually come up with a few dollars to buy a hamburger at the host restaurant. You will usually get a better turn out at fund raising activities if you focus on the purpose that the money raised will be used for. Most of us do not get excited about washing cars, but we do get excited about a trip to an amusement park youth conference or Bible camp.

Building Character in Teenagers

"Then David said, This is the house of the Lord God, and this is the altar of the burnt offering for Israel. And David commanded to gather together the strangers that were in the land of Israel; and he set masons to hew wrought stones to build the house of God. And David prepared iron in abundance for the nails for the doors of the gates, and for the joinings; and brass in abundance without weight; also cedar trees in abundance: for the Zidonians and they of Tyre brought much cedar wood to David. And David said, Solomon my son is young and tender, and the house that is to be builded for the Lord must be exceeding magnifical, of fame and of glory throughout all countries: I will therefore now make preparation for it. So David prepared abundantly before his death. Then he called for Solomon his son, and charged him to build an house for the Lord God of Israel."

I Chronicles 22:1-6

To this point we have discussed the importance of leadership, organizing the youth ministry, prospecting and winning teens to Christ. This is the preparation work for the building of the Temple. In the Old Testament the Temple was the dwelling place of God. Since Calvary the Christian has become the Temple, the dwelling place of God. Thus the ministry of building Character in young people is the work of building the Temple, i.e. building the person.

Christian parents have a responsibility to build character in their children. *"And, ye fathers, provoke not your children to wrath: but bring them up in the nurture and admonition of the Lord."* (Ephesians 6:4) The local church, through sound Bible teaching and preaching, edifies what the parents are doing in the home in building character in their children. Then we have the parents who are not Christians, the parents who have little if any character. The church must reach these children with the gospel of Jesus Christ and disciple them. You see, dear friend, the youth ministry is the business of salvaging, rescuing, recycling, building, and re-building people.

In First Chronicles 22:1-5, we have a wonderful illustration of building character in young people. David the king announced that the Temple to be built for God should be *"exceeding magnifical"*. He then acquired all of the tools, materials, and laborers to build the Temple, *("I will therefore now make preparation for it")*. Then David told his Son Solomon to build the Temple. How well that describes the responsibility of parents and the church in building character in young people. Our responsibility is to provide the materials, the tools, and we must be the laborers; but we must also teach young people to "*add thereto*".

1) It is our Responsibility to teach them to add Character to themselves.

David told Solomon in verse fourteen, *"Now, behold, in my trouble I have prepared for the house of the Lord an hundred thousand talents of gold, and a thousand thousand talents of silver; and of brass and iron without weight; for it is in abundance: timber also and stone have I prepared; and thou mayest add thereto."* Our own children will not always be under our influence and the young people we work with through the church ministry are not always under our influence either. The key then to building character is to teach young people to add character to their own lives. They must learn to seek God's will, to search out the Scriptures when making decisions, choosing friends, establishing relationships with people of the opposite sex, choosing a spouse, finding employment, and every other aspect of life. In our example of building the Temple, everything needed was provided, but the instruction was for Solomon to add thereto. We are responsible to provide the things necessary to build the temple and to teach young people to build their own character, and then challenge them to *"add thereto"*.

2) Teach them to Work.

Building anything of value requires work. We have reared a generation in America that looks for more ways to avoid work than they do to find work. May I add here that work should not be a method of punishment! Junior should not be made to clean out the garage because he was disobedient, he should have the privilege of cleaning out the garage because work is character, work is pleasure, and work is Biblical. Many have the idea that to have an effective youth ministry they must entertain the young people at every activity. This philosophy may bring in a number of teenagers to attend a ball game or pizza party but it does not build an effective youth ministry. It does not produce character or responsible teenagers. The youth ministry is not an entertainment business; it is a ministry, which should produce laborers for the cause of Christ, adults who are involved in the ministries of their church, soul winners, leaders, and people of strong Christian character. I submit to you that you cannot teach young people character without teaching them how to work. So instead of the monthly visit to the amusement park, how about if you have an activity at the church such as a workday!

The teenagers can clean out the church's storage room, they can paint a Sunday school classroom, they can weed the flowers around the building, and they can decorate for the mission conference. There are many "work projects" they can take on that they will enjoy doing as they fellowship with other young people, serve the Lord and learn character in the process while doing something they can be proud of when they are finished.

3) Teach them to Minister to others.

Nothing builds character more than learning to serve others. There are many areas of service teenagers can take part in that will help develop character as they help meet the needs of others. For example the teen ministry could minister to a widow by raking her yard, cleaning her windows, cutting firewood, and preparing a nice meal which they would enjoy with her over a time of fellowship. Of course these things could be done for widowers, shut-ins and other folks with special needs. The teens could visit shut-ins and take them a preaching tape of the pastor from a recent church service and sing some songs to them while visiting. Cookies could be baked as an activity and then distributed to the residents of a local nursing home. The teens could sing some gospel hymns to the residents and fellowship for a while. The nursing home ministry is a wonderful ministry for the teens to be involved in.

4) Character is Keeping Priorities in Order.

A job at a fast food restaurant is never more important than Sunday morning church, Sunday night church or Wednesday night prayer meeting. These establishments that hire teenagers are looking for young people of character and are happy to work with the church schedule if they are able to have a dependable employee. Encourage your teenagers who want to get jobs, or whose parents require them to get jobs, to tell the prospective employer in the job interview that they cannot work Sundays or Wednesday nights. If the employer is unwilling to hire them on that basis, assure the young person that another employer will. Our first obligation is to the Lord Jesus Christ, not the fast food industry.

A topic of continual teaching to teenagers should be that of personal devotions. Encourage them to begin each day with Bible reading and prayer time. Others topics of character should be taught in Bible lessons such as character in finances, honor to parents, and showing respect to those in authority. Also teach Gods plan in girl friend boy friend relationships such as, courting, marriage and then sex.

5) Applaud Character.

Our society has measured success in wealth, athletic ability and talent instead of in character and Biblical morals. Often on Sunday morning we applaud the teenage boy who scored the most points for the high school basketball team, who afterwards went out and got drunk. And we overlook the fourteen-year-old bus kid that has been getting himself out of bed every Sunday morning for three years so he could be in church. He is putting forth his very best effort to serve the Lord while living in a very difficult situation at home. He reads his Bible each day; he prays each morning for his drunkard father's salvation; he wins souls; he is faithful to church; he is respectful and has already surrendered to preach. The problem is he can't dribble a basketball. Dear friend we applaud the wrong one. I'm not saying there is anything wrong with applauding ones effort and success in sports. I am saying let us not overlook character. Applaud athletic ability in its proper place and applaud character above sports. Let us put our emphasis on character and serving God. Let's put more emphasis on serving others, winning souls, being in the Lord's work, reading the Bible, prayer and victorious Christian living than we do on entertainment, sports and talent! Applaud what is done for God! Make Christian character the goal to strive for!

Counseling Teenagers

"And the asses of Kish Saul's father were lost. And Kish said to Saul his son, Take now one of the servants with thee, and arise, go seek the asses. And he passed through Mount Ephraim, and passed through the land of Shalisha, but they found them not: then they passed through the Land of Shalim, and there they were not: and he passed through the Land of the Benjamites, but they found them not. And when they were come to the land of Zuph, Saul said to his servant that was with him, Come, and let us return; lest my father leave caring for the asses, and take thought for us. And he said unto him, Behold now, there is in this city a man of God, and he is an honourable man; all that he saith cometh surely to pass: now let us go thither; peradventure he can shew us our way that we should go."
I Samuel 9:3-6

"Without counsel purposes are disappointed: but in the multitude of counsellors they are established."
Proverbs 15:22

Teenagers face problems today like no other generation has had to deal with. Many young people have serious family problems for which they need counsel and edification and Bible answers. There are other situations, teens face for which they need Biblical counsel. In our text in First Samuel we see that Saul sought the counsel of the man of God for the direction he should take, *"peradventure he can shew us our way that we should go."*

I agree that most counseling should be done from the pulpit to the pew with Bible preaching. However, local church pastors and youth leaders must understand that teenagers sometimes need one on one counsel from the man of God to determine the way that they should go. If we do not meet this need for counsel through the local church, young people will go to their friends and public school counselors for what often turns out to be un-biblical counsel which only leads to more problems. Giving Biblical counsel is part of ministering to the needs of young people. The following are some practical principles and procedures in counseling teenagers.

1) When Counseling, Depend upon the Lord.

"Trust in the Lord with all thine heart; and lean not unto thine own understanding. In all thy ways acknowledge him, and he shall direct thy paths." Proverbs 3:5-6

The ultimate goal in Biblical counseling is to teach people to get their answers from the Lord. Never allow them to become dependent upon you, but teach them to go to the Word of God and to seek the Lord in prayer. In order for the counselor to teach this principle to the people he counsels he must rely on the Lord himself when giving counsel. In his book, *Competent to Counsel,* Dr. Jay Adams says, "Counseling is the work of the Holy Spirit. Effective counseling cannot be done apart from Him. He is called the Paraclete (counselor) who in Christ's place came to be another counselor of the same sort that Christ had been to His disciples."

It is best to begin the counseling session in prayer with the counselee, asking the Lord for wisdom and direction in attaining the decision that will glorify the Lord Jesus Christ. God is not the author of confusion; he will give us guidance. Matthew 7:7 says, *"Ask, and it shall be given you; seek, and ye shall find; knock, and it shall be opened unto you:"* It is also wise to pray with the counselee at the close of the counseling session, asking the Lord to help the counselee follow through with whatever needs to be done to achieve what God wants accomplished in their life.

Follow the Holy Spirit's leading when giving counsel. God's wisdom is available to us. James 1:5 says, *"If any of you lack wisdom, let him ask of God, that giveth to all men liberally, and upbraideth not; and it shall be given him."* So let us be diligent to seek his wisdom that we may be helpful in giving direction to those in our care.

2) Is the Counselee a Christian?

One of the most important questions to ask a counselee is if they are born again. It is good to do this by asking them to share with you the testimony of their conversion. If they cannot give you a clear testimony of their salvation it could be that they are not saved or that they are unclear about salvation. You cannot help them with any other problems or decisions until the issue of salvation is settled.

3) Be a Good Listener.

James 1:19 tells us, *"Wherefore, my beloved bretheren, let every man be swift to hear, slow to speak, slow to wrath:"* Listening is one of the most important aspects of counseling. Letting people talk out their problems will often help them find the answer on their own. Listening will also enable you to cover any objections they may bring up concerning the counsel you give them. For example if a young person shares with you that they recently got into some trouble while with a "friend" and you share with them that they may be running with the wrong crowd. They may object that they like their friends and that, their friends care about them. You would then remind them that they told you they were with one of these "friends" when they got into trouble. Listening closely as they talk to you will also help them better understand and accept the counsel you give to them, because you will have listened intently to the situation.

4) Give Biblical Counsel

What we think or what our opinion is; is not as important as what the word of God says about any issue. In giving counsel it is important to stress to the counselee what the Bible says concerning their situation or dilemma by showing them specific scripture. The Bible is where the answer to all of mankind's questions and problems are. By giving Bible counsel we are teaching the counselee to go to the Word of God for answers, we are teaching them to get their answers from the Bible in the future.

5) Develop Bible "Formulas"

If you became ill and went to the doctor, the doctor might give you a medical prescription for whatever ailed you. This medical prescription would most likely be a composition of various medicines and herbs that would formulate into a remedy to help you with your ailment. The Bible has formulas that are remedies for the souls and lives of men. For example, God's grace with man's faith in the Lord Jesus Christ and his finished work at Calvary brings salvation to man.

When a young person comes to you for counsel concerning a matter, it is best to use scripture to point them to a Biblical formula to their problem. For example, let's say a teenager comes to you with a family problem. Maybe they are rebelling against their parents in some area; maybe they do not like the rules mom and dad have put down in the home. I have developed a Bible formula to give them.

Formula for a Teenager that is Rebellious.

The Bible says in Ephesians 6:1-2 *"Children, obey your parents in the Lord: for this is right. Honour thy father and mother; which is the first commandment with promise;"*

There are no requirements that the parents must meet in order to have their children obey them. The Bible does not say obey your parents "IF" they buy you the car you want, the clothes you want, the tennis shoes you want, or let you have the friends you want. The Bible says, "Obey your parents in the Lord." If your parents are not what they should be or what you want them to be, you still obey them. You obey them not because of who they are or are not. You obey them, "in the Lord". You obey them because God commands it. Then there is the command to honor our parents. The word honor has three great applications.

A) Honor them in their Old Age.
Some day our parents may become more dependent on us than we are on them. When and if this happens we should care for them. That is honor.

B) Honor their Name.
In other words, have a good testimony. No matter what your parent's lives may be like, you can still honor them by having a good testimony.

C) Honor is the Right Attitude in Obedience.

To obey with a wrong attitude, complaining and whining all while we are obeying is not honor, it is dishonor. To honor our parents is to obey them with the right attitude.

I would also share with a teenager who may not have a good family situation that there are no perfect families, parents or children. That we are to love the one we have; be the best son or daughter we can be; and that God always blesses obedience to his word.

6) Do not Condemn Them.

They may have a drunkard dad, or they may not even know their dad. Their mother may be a prostitute, a drug addict, their life may be difficult and they are trying to find their way. We are not their judges. Our responsibility is to show them the way to victory, to show them the way that they should go. We cannot help them by condemning them but we can help them by telling them of God's grace and victory.

7) Have Compassion.

"And of some have compassion, making a difference:"

Jude 22

In John chapter eight verses one through eleven we read about the scribes and Pharisees bringing a woman to the Lord Jesus Christ that was caught in the act of adultery. They brought her to Jesus to test him, to see what he would do. This woman was brought to Christ in her shame, with repentance. She stood in His presence before the whole crowd of people. The thing that Jesus did was have compassion on her. He did not humiliate her any further, but rather he stooped down to the ground and, I believe, he listed the sins of the scribes and the Pharisees in the ground. The Bible then says in John 8:7, *"So when they continued asking him, he lifted up himself, and said unto them, He that is without sin among you, let him first cast a stone at her."* Dear friend, this was an act of compassion. Correction or discipline without compassion is vengeance. We find several places in the Bible where Jesus was, *"...moved with compassion on them"*, and *"...moved with compassion toward them"*. To have compassion is to feel sympathy or pity, but may I take the definition a little further using Jesus as our example? Compassion in action is loving someone in the situation they are in and having a desire to help them rise above that situation. This is what Jesus does, He loves people where they are, and he loves us in our sin and offers us salvation. He loves us when we stumble and backslide and forgives us in our confession.

In counseling we must express genuine concern and compassion, not seeing the counselee as they are, but as they can be.

8) When the Problem is Sin.

There are times when counseling is necessary because a young person is seeking direction about a decision they are making, or they need counsel on how to deal with a certain situation. There are other times when counsel is needed because the counselee has gotten involved in sin. When this is the case the counselor must be compassionate, but he must also be stern and direct. Dr. Jay Adams in his book, The Christian Counselor's Manuel states, "Christian counselors should not need to be reminded that they have been called to labor in opposition to the world, the flesh, and the devil. He further states, "Counseling, therefore, must be understood and conducted as a spiritual battle." Therefore, when counseling a young person about a sin problem, show them from scripture what the Bible says concerning the sin, let the word of God be their judge and you be their counselor. And then show them scripture concerning how to obtain victory over the sin. The purpose of counseling a teenager about a sin problem is to give them a solution to the problem.

Keep in mind that some teens may get under conviction about their sin after hearing a sermon that God used to reveal that sin to them. So counsel should be given them compassionately and in meekness, leading them to confess and forsake the sin, to put the sin behind them, to "leave it at the altar". Forgiveness comes through confession, but victory comes through forsaking the sin. Isaiah 55:7 says, *"Let the wicked forsake his way, and the unrighteous man his thoughts: and let him return unto the Lord, and he will have mercy upon him; and to our God, for he will abundantly pardon."*

9) Do not Reveal Confidences.

"The words of a talebearer are as wounds, and they go down into the innermost parts of the belly." Proverbs 18:8

If the counselee tells you something in confidence, keep it in confidence. If they find out that you have revealed what they have told you in confidence, you will lose their trust and be unable to help them. Others will also lose trust in you and will not come to you when they are in need of counsel.

10) Know When to Refer.

I firmly believe that the Spirit-filled, Bible believing man of God is completely qualified to give counsel to people with problems. I further believe that a non-believing psychiatrist, psychologist or "professional counselor" is not qualified to give my dog a biscuit. I also believe it is wise for the church pastor to do the counseling of his people, including the teenagers. Outside of a teenager asking general Bible questions of the youth leader or Sunday school teacher, the Pastor should be involved in any counsel of a serious matter. However the inexperienced pastor, youth leader or Christian layman should refer difficult situations and problems he is not confident he can help with to a more experienced pastor.

The Counselor should Refer:

A) When the counselee is suicidal.

B) When the counselee is homicidal

C) When the counselor sees that the situation is beyond his ability.

D) When the counselor realizes the situation is beyond his time limit.

E) When the situation is medical.

F) When a serious crime has been committed.

11) Always Seek to Restore.

"Brethren, if a man be overtaken in a fault, ye which are spiritual, restore such an one in the spirit of meekness; considering thyself, lest thou also be tempted."

Galatians 6:1

God is in the business of salvaging, recycling and restoring. God forgives and God forgets. The purpose of counseling the teenager that has gotten into sin is to restore them to fellowship in the Lord, to help them set boundaries to keep them from making the same mistake twice. Galatians chapter six, verse one gives us the perfect formula for restoration in counseling. First of all notice the offense *"overtaken in a fault"* the word fault here describes a transgression, a sin. It does not measure the transgression. It does not say that there is a certain size of *"fault"* that can be restored and another size that cannot be restored. Because, there is no transgression a Christian can commit; but that God cannot restore them. Next notice who is responsible for the one *"overtaken in a fault"*, it is *"ye which are spiritual"*. The leader is the spiritual one, the pastor, the youth leader, the Sunday school teacher; they are to be the spiritual. Now notice the assignment given to the spiritual one (the leader), *"Restore such an one in the spirit of meekness."* How precious is the word *"restore"*, which God uses to describe the work to be done here for the fallen! To restore is to repair, or to put back to the original condition.

Dear Friend, when the need arises to help a fallen Christian that has been overtaken in a fault. Let us reach out to them in the spirit of meekness, considering that it could be us, that has fallen, that we may have compassion enough to lead them to restoration. Let us remember that God restored Elijah, Jonah, the Apostle Peter and many others in the Bible. They were all greatly used of God to do mighty works in his name after their restoration.

12) Precautions to take when Counseling.

The pastor or youth leader that counsels with people today needs to be very cautious about where, how and with whom they counsel. The following are some safeguards to take when in counseling sessions.

A) Never record counseling sessions mechanically.

It is best to keep brief hand written notes listing the date and topic discussed. Keep these records in a concealed location under lock and key.

B) Never counsel the opposite sex alone.

The wise pastor or youth leader will have his wife or other godly woman present when counseling a lady of any age, especially a teenage girl. It is just as unwise to counsel with a teenager of the same sex alone. It is understandable for the counselee to want to speak personally with the counselor, but there should always be another person within visual distance of the counselor and counselee.

C) The counselor should never touch the counselee for any reason.

Touching could be misinterpreted by the counselee, and could bring temptation to the counselor that could destroy his ministry and hurt the life of the counselee.

D) Consult with the parents of teenagers to whom you counsel with on serious matters.

If a teenager comes to you for counsel whom you do not know, it is wise to ask if their parents know that they were coming to you for counsel and to consult with the parents if you are going to counsel them more than one time.

E) Most counseling should be done by appointment.

When someone comes to you for counsel concerning a non-pressing matter it is wise to set an appointment. Scheduling an appointment enables the counselor to prepare himself spiritually for the counseling session, to prayerfully consider the person's life and to control the counseling process from the very beginning. If a counselee has an urgent matter for which they need counsel it is wise to locate an appropriate place and atmosphere in which to speak with them.

F) Choose the place of counseling carefully.

The pastor and or youth leader should have his office in an appropriate situation for counseling. It is wise to have a window on the office door and to have plenty of good lighting. The seating arrangement for counseling sessions should be appropriate, comfortable, and professional. In some counseling situations it is advisable for the counselor to sit across a table from the counselee. This would be appropriate when giving counsel concerning helping a person overcome sin in their life or in helping someone put their life back in order or in counseling situations that would require helping the counselee put together a plan of action to deal with their problem. I refer to this as instructional counseling. In situations where the purpose of the counseling session is to console or to help make a decision it would not be inappropriate for the counselor to sit facing the counselee in comfortable chairs.

13) When a Parent seeks Counsel for their Teenager.

From time to time a parent will bring a teenager to the pastor or youth leader for counseling. This may be due to some rebellion in the teenager, or it may be because the teenager has recently had a difficult experience such as the death of a friend, parent or grandparent. It may be due to one of the parents leaving the home; a serious illness has come to a family member; or other problem that lays heavy on the teenager's heart. In other instances it may be that the parent lacks parenting skills and is having trouble with their teen as a result.

In all of these situations it is often good for the teenager if the counselor schedules two to four counseling sessions with the teenager. I would recommend that the parent come on the counseling sessions for two reasons. First of all this gets the parent(s) involved in resolving the problem. Secondly, if through counseling the teenager it becomes obvious that the parent(s) need counsel in Biblical parenting skills, you could have them come into your office after each counseling session with the teenager and share some Bible principles on rearing teenagers while the teenager waits in another room.

For the young youth leader that feels the parents need some counsel on parenting, it would be wise to involve the pastor in the counseling sessions or to seek his guidance in helping the teenager and the parent(s). If the problem is behavioral on the teenager's part, the counselor should meet with the teenager, the parent(s) and then both parties together so they can work together to resolve the problem, sharing with the teenager what his or her Biblical responsibility is in resolving the problem. Never discuss the parent's lack of parenting skills in the presence of their teenager. But there may be situations when in a counseling session that the parent may need to confess to the teenager that they have not been the kind of parent they should be and that they are willing to do whatever is necessary to Biblically resolve the problem. Do not try to place blame on either party for the problems in the parent-teenager relationship. It is better to use the counseling sessions to teach what the Biblical solutions are in resolving the problems.

14) Counseling Sessions should not be Continual.

The purpose of counseling is not to teach the counselee to depend upon the counselor but to depend upon the Lord. The Freudian philosophy of a lifetime of counseling and psychotherapy is not Biblical but rather it is against everything the Bible teaches. The counseling process consists of three fundamental and Biblical steps. First determine what the problem is, secondly find the Bible solution, and thirdly help the counselee Biblically resolve the problem. This may take a few more than three counseling sessions for a serious problem, but when the

Lord is involved in solving our problems it does not take a lifetime. Jesus Christ solved our biggest problem in three days, when he died on Calvary for our sin and when he arose victoriously over death, Hell, and the grave three days later.

15) The Counselor must keep his Personal walk with Christ Fresh.

Any Christian that is used of God to give Bible counsel should have daily Bible reading, study, and meditation as well as a daily time of precious fellowship with the Lord in prayer.

Reaching Rebellious Teens

"Notwithstanding the children rebelled against me: they walked not in my statutes, neither kept my judgments to do them, which if a man do, he shall even live in them; they polluted my sabbaths: then I said, I would pour out my fury upon them, to accomplish my anger against them in the wilderness." Ezekiel 20:21

People have been rebelling against God and authority since Adam and Eve rebelled against God in the Garden of Eden. Young people from good Christian homes will sometimes rebel and even break the hearts of their parents, pastor, and Christian friends. The worst thing we can do with a rebellious young person is to do nothing; we must do something, but what do we do?

I do not know that I have all of the answers but I do have some Bible principles that may be helpful. Before I share them allow me to make some observations about rebellion in young people.

1) Rebellion is Natural but it is not acceptable.

God did not accept it in Adam and Eve, nor did He accept it in several other people in the Bible. We cannot accept it either; we cannot overlook it. Parents that have a rebellious teen cannot overlook rebellious behavior in their son or daughter as they try to convince themselves that it is just a phase young people go through. Rebellion is a problem that must be dealt with Biblically.

2) Rebellion is the result of a Spiritual Problem.

The spiritual problem could be that the young person is not saved. It could be that they have bitterness in their heart toward someone who has done something to them. It could be pride, anger, selfishness, or some other sin in their heart that they have not dealt with.

3) Rebellion could be a result of the Company they are keeping.

Friendship is one of the strongest influences a young person has in his or her life. Negative associations with peers or ungodly friends can and will produce rebellion. Using God's response to Adam and Eve's rebellion against his word in the Garden of Eden, let us see how we can attempt to reach the rebellious teenager.

A) Confront the Rebellious Teenager.
"And the Lord God called unto Adam, and said unto him, Where art thou?" Genesis 3:9

God confronted Adam about his rebellion, asking him where he was, and who had told him that he was naked. God also questioned Adam about the forbidden tree, *"Hast thou eaten of the tree, whereof I commanded thee that thou shouldest not eat?"* The rebellious young person must be confronted about his behavior. Questions must be asked about the influences he is listening to. Adam and Eve listened to Satan. The rebellious teen is listening to someone that is influencing their behavior. Disappointment must be expressed to the young person that rebellion is not acceptable behavior; that you are concerned about them getting into serious trouble if they do not make things right.

B) Love them, but not their Rebellion.

God was not pleased with Adam's rebellion but He still loved Adam and Eve enough to provide coats of skin for a covering for them. We cannot cover up rebellion but we must love the rebellious one if we are to help them.

C) Work with their Parents.

If the young person is in your church youth ministry, you should have some kind of relationship with their parents. Even if the parents do not attend the church, you should still know them. Approach the parents about the concerns you have for their child's rebellious behavior. It could be that the parents want your input and help but do not know how to ask. If you get a good reception and response from the parents you may want to try and get the parents and the rebellious young person to talk with you together. You may be able to win the lost parent to Christ and help the whole family situation. The parents may be a key factor in reaching the rebellious teenager and getting him or her, turned around.

D) Be Committed to helping the Rebellious young person.

"Unto Adam also and to his wife did the Lord God make coats of skins, and clothed them." Genesis 3:21

The sacrifice of an animal was made to clothe Adam and Eve; I believe it was a lamb that was sacrificed. If we are going to reach a rebellious young person, sacrifices and commitments must be made. A parent may need to make some major changes to recapture the heart of their son or daughter. They may have to move and / or change jobs in order to be home more. They may have to sacrifice material things in order to have time to invest in rescuing their teenager. The pastor or youth leader that is trying to reach a rebellious young person will need to be willing to make some commitments as well. Commitments to invest time with the young person; calling them on the phone and sending them notes to let them know that you are praying for them and that you have not given up on them.

E) Control the Environment of the Rebellious young person.

Do not allow the rebellious teen to brag about his or her rebellion, or to gloat in his or her bad behavior. It is not wise to allow him or her to control the environment at youth activities or gatherings with any inappropriate conversations or behavior. Rebellious teens often like to do these things to draw attention to themselves and to express their rebellion openly before their peers. Keep in mind that God completely changed Adam and Eve's environment when they rebelled against His Word. He put them out of the Garden of Eden. A rebellious young person when given the opportunity to influence other young people will produce more rebellious young people.

F) Do not constantly remind the rebellious young person of their rebellion.

But focus instead on the potential that they have and what their rebellion is costing them.

G) Control your own actions when conversing and dealing with a rebellious young person.

If you yell, they will yell. Be firm but be in control. Do not re-act to their behavior, but act upon what is right.

H) Do not compromise your principles or youth ministry standards in an attempt "to get them back".

The object is not to make them happy, but to help them get right.

I) Pray for them and with them!

God can get a hold of their heart so don't ever give up on them, no matter what they do. Continue to pray for them and love them. Every time you see them pray with them and tell them that you are praying for them.

J) Do not refer to the rebellious young person in a negative way to their face or to others.

You will only push them away further by referring to them as the "black sheep", the "wayward teen", or the "prodigal teen".

K) Do not stop being their pastor or youth leader.

Just today I spoke on the phone with the pastor of a church in a northern state who shared with me that he had "written off" several young people who had once attended his church. How sad it is to hear such words coming from a pastor! I am so glad that our Heavenly Father never writes us off or gives up on us and we should never give up hope on anyone either. We will have a much better chance of eventually reaching the rebellious young person if they are able to say, "My pastor never gave up on me, even when I was on the bottom." Or "My youth leader never wrote me off, though others did, my youth leader stayed with me and kept praying, calling and visiting me. I know he cared."

L) Welcome them back with open arms.

When the rebellious young person returns as the prodigal son did to his father, with genuine repentance, and a spirit of surrender, welcome him back with an open heart, complete forgiveness, and restoration.

Helping Troubled Teens

"...a broken spirit drieth the bones." Proverbs 17:22b

"Heaviness in the heart of man maketh it stoop:"
Proverbs 12:25a

Let me begin this chapter by defining what I mean by a "Troubled Teen". Webster's dictionary defines "troubled" as, to worry or grieve, to disturb mentally, misfortune, a difficult situation, social disturbances. I would describe a troubled teen as one that has emotional and behavioral problems that are derived from a lack of parental guidance and attention. Young people that have numerous family problems and come from an "environmentally dysfunctional" home life usually live with a *"heaviness in the heart"*.

Other teens can become troubled when a change has taken place in their life that has left them with a feeling of insecurity or resentment such as a parent leaving the home, a dad losing his job or a move to a new area. The suicide of a friend or acquaintance is always troublesome to a teenager. A teenager from a good home that begins to associate with the wrong circle of influence will become troubled.

We reap in the lives of our young people today the seed that has been sown in our society for over thirty years now; with the breakdown of the family; the watering down of Biblical standards and convictions; rebellion against God and righteousness in the leadership of our country. May I also add to these, a weakness in many pulpits across America to preach *"thus saith the Lord"*! The issue at hand is; how do we help emotionally troubled teenagers! Let us consider some "troubled teen" situations and what we can do to help.

1) How to help young people with Developmental Emotional problems. This would include the Mentally Handicapped.

A) Love them, as they are, their heavenly Father does.

B) Help them reach their individual potential.

C) Protect them from the cruelty of others.

D) Understand that they need special help and attention.

2) Emotional Problems that produce disruptive behavior.

A) Understand what the Behavior is saying.
"I want someone to love me; I want to feel important; I want to be noticed; I want attention; and I want hope." Most troubled teenagers will accept negative attention over no attention at all.

B) Some behavioral problems are an attempt on the young person's part to have control.
This is usually due to having no liberty to express their emotions in their home.

C) A behavioral problem in which a young person hurts others verbally or physically is usually an outward expression of the hurt they have inside. They may have anger toward a parent that verbally or physically abuses them or has abandoned them and they are seeking vengeance. Ephesians 6:4 warns us, "... provoke not your children to wrath." Wrath is an anger that seeks vengeance.

D) Behavioral problems in many troubled young people, is usually a crying out to see if anyone loves them.

3) How we can Help!

A) Pray for them and with them.

B) Love them unconditionally.

C) Give them a sense of belonging, give them some meaningful responsibility or task in the church or on a youth outing.

D) Give them a sense of worth. Hearing statements like, "I am glad you are part of our church, It's good to see you today; I'm glad we are friends"; and, "You did a good job;" on a regular basis can make a big difference in the lives of many troubled young people. *"Heaviness in the heart of man maketh it stoop: but a good word maketh it glad."*

Proverbs 12:25

E) Give them your time.

F) Proper nutrition can often have a calming effect, discuss their diet with them and encourage them to eat healthy, less sugar more vegetables.

4) How to help in a Classroom setting.

A) Anticipate the problem and prepare your heart to deal with it in a spirit of compassion and resolve.

B) Place "troubled young people" near the leader and try to do so without drawing negative attention to them.

C) Maintain control of the group.

D) Remain in control of yourself, if you lose control of your own actions, the class gains control of you.

5) Home lives that Produce Emotional and Behavioral Problems.

A) No Dad in the home.

B) No Mom in the home.

C) Alcoholism in the home.

D) Drug abuse in the home.

E) Mental and emotional abuse in the home; the young person being told that they are not wanted; that they are stupid or worthless.

F) Poverty in the home, this can produce feelings in the young person that they are not as valuable as other young people are.

G) Improper diet in the home. Parents who feed their children sweets and starches with little if any vegetables and grains will have some behavioral problems in their children.

H) Sexual abuse. This causes a young person to feel "dirty"; more like an object than a person; insecure and in continual fear.

I) Physical abuse. This also produces fear, vengeance and insecurity in the heart of a young person.

6) How to Help Young People with Problems in their Home Life.

A) Pray with Them and for Them.

A prayer with them similar to this; "Lord Jesus, thank you for sending Joe to our church. He is a fine young man and I know you have a great plan for his life. Help him to do your will and to honor you in all that he does. Lord, we love him and we are thankful that you are doing a great work in his life even now. Help me to be a blessing to him, as he is to me. Amen" This kind of prayer will help you express to the young person that you see their potential and it will help them because they are hearing you tell God what you see in them.

B) Stand in the gap and make up the hedge where the "dysfunctional family" is lacking.

C) Love them and let them hear it and see it without anything being expected of them in return.

D) Focus on their strengths not on their weaknesses.

E) Give them a sense of belonging. A church and youth ministry with a family atmosphere will help accomplish this.

F) Teach them Bible truth about the family, drugs, alcohol genuine love, and God's word concerning sexual relationships.

G) Help them set goals that they can realistically achieve. When they achieve them, let them know that you knew they could, that you believed in their ability.

H) Praise them publicly.

I) Scold them privately and lovingly.

J) Be patient with them, their problems have been developing over years, it will take time to make progress.

K) If they "unload" on you, don't take it personal.
They may have a lot bottled up in them and they probably have never had someone they could trust before. Most of the people in their life, who were supposed to love them, have hurt them.

L) Help them to deal with bitterness, and teach them Bible principles of forgiveness, even of parents.

M) Be the example of a Christian that they need in the world.

N) Attempt to win their parents to Christ.
Nothing can transform their lives like their salvation and the salvation of their family.

O) Get them in the Bible by giving them Bible answers to every question they ask, and by showing them from scripture how to deal with their problems. Use the scripture to show them God loves them and to give them assurance of salvation and of the love that Christ has for them.

Reaching Families Through Teenagers

"Now the man out of whom the devils were departed besought him that he might be with him: but Jesus sent him away, saying, Return to thine own house, and shew how great things God hath done unto thee. And he went his way, and published throughout the whole city how great things Jesus had done unto him." Luke 8:38-39

The Bible does not specifically state that the maniac of Gadera had a family but I believe that he did based on Jesus telling him in our text, *"Return to thine own house."* And in Mark's gospel we read the words of Jesus to the man, *"Go home to thy friends."* One of the most important things we can do after winning someone to Christ is to go to their house and try to win their entire family to Christ. Families can be reached for the Saviour if we will reach out to the parents of the children and teenagers who ride our church buses, come to our services and attend youth activities.

The following are some methods of reaching families through the young people we already have in our church and those we win to Christ.

1) Make a point to introduce yourself to the parents of the young people you work with in your church.

The first time you go to visit a young person who has attended a church service or youth activity, introduce yourself to their parents. Thank them for allowing their teenager to attend your church. Compliment the parents on their son or daughter's behavior.

2) Build a rapport with the parent.

Find a common ground, and compliment their home or something in their home that you can discuss with them to help them feel comfortable talking with you.

3) Tell them about their son or daughter's salvation if they accepted Christ while at your church service or youth activity.

Use discretion and wisdom in doing this. You may say something like this. "Mr. Jones, we appreciate you allowing Judy to attend our service Sunday night. Following the service, Judy spoke with one of our ladies about her relationship with Jesus Christ. After she was shown some scripture, Judy prayed and trusted Jesus Christ as her personal Saviour. We wanted to share this exciting news with you."

4) Responses and Objections from parents and how to deal with them.

When you share with some parents that their teenager has made a profession of faith in Jesus Christ, anything can happen, you may get a good response from the parents or you may get a negative response. Not all parents are going to get excited about their teenager getting a "new religion" and some will have other objections. Some of these responses and objections can be dealt with successfully if handled properly and with the right attitude.

To accomplish this, remember three important things. One, be polite in your response, never rude or self-righteous. Secondly, keep in mind that your purpose is to win the parents to Christ, not to win an argument. If you cannot win the parents to Christ on this visit keep the door open for an opportunity to return. Your secondary purpose is to get the teenager baptized and in church. If you argue with the parents, you may win the argument, but you will lose the teenager. Thirdly, you represent Jesus Christ, therefore be a good representative and keep a positive attitude.

The following are some responses and objections you may encounter from parents and suggestions on how to deal with them.

A) Parent's response, "We have our own religion."
Rebuttal, "Yes, Mr. Jones, Judy shared that with us and that is wonderful. It is also all the more reason we were excited that Judy now has a personal relationship with Jesus Christ as we know from scripture we all can have."

B) Parent's response, "With all of the trouble she has been in, she needs religion."
Rebuttal, "Mr. Jones, I appreciate the concern you have for your daughter, and I know how difficult it is to rear teenagers today. That is the reason we wanted to share with you that Judy has taken this important step in trusting Christ as her Saviour. We also wanted to share with you that we have a very active youth ministry and we want to help enforce your efforts by encouraging Judy to make the right choices in life."

C) Parent's response, "We have our own church, if Judy wants to go to church then she can go to our family church."

Rebuttal, "It is wonderful that you have a good church. Because you do have a church and realize how important it is to have a personal relationship with Jesus Christ, and since Judy is not currently attending your church would you object if she visits ours?"

Parent's response: "I am an Atheist and I don't want my children to have anything to do with religion."

Rebuttal: "I'm sorry you feel that way Mr. Jones, I wish there was a way I could persuade you to change your mind about the Lord. But may I ask, would you object to giving Judy the opportunity to decide for herself?" (We would never advise a parent to let their children decide for themselves, whether or not they want to attend church, but when dealing with an atheist we will make an exception.)

5) If the response is positive from the parents, witness to them.

If they do trust Christ as their Saviour, ask for permission for their son or daughter to be baptized. If the parents agree to the baptism, invite the entire family to come to the service.

6) If you do not win the parents to Christ on the first visit.

Work towards building a relationship with them. Stop by and visit from time to time and watch for opportunities to witness to them again.

7) Helping Christian teenagers reach their lost parents.

A) Teach and encourage the teenagers to be a good Christian example in their home by obeying their parents, honoring them and keeping a good attitude toward them.

B) Teach the teenagers to be a good Christian example by having daily devotional time of Bible reading and prayer time. Also, encourage the teenagers to not watch improper television programs and video movies with their parents by politely asking to be excused to their room.

C) Visit the teenager's family routinely. Be polite, enthusiastic and compliment the parents on their teenager's behavior. Thank them for allowing their son or daughter to attend your church. Statements to the parents like, "We really enjoy having John attend the church, and it's obvious that he has been taught how to behave and how to be respectful" will enhance the relationship.

D) Personally invite the parents to all special services, especially Mothers day, Fathers day, Easter, and Christmas. Share with the parents that you know, "It would mean a lot to John if you would surprise him and be in Church on Father's day," or, "Mr. and Mrs. Jones, it would mean a lot to John if you could see him in the Easter Program. He has worked very hard and I know he loves you."

It is easier to persuade parents in this manner when you have worked hard yourself to build a relationship with them and have proven to them, through your faithfulness, that you care about their son or daughter.

8) Have events specially designated to reach parents.

A) Mother-daughter Banquet.

Invite the mother of every teenager in the church to attend. Make a special effort to invite the lost mothers of your teenagers. Let them know it will be a special time to give them honor and that they will receive a special gift. Do it first class with a nice meal and have the room appropriately decorated with a motherly theme. In would not be inappropriate to have a lady speak and then have the pastor bring a salvation message, giving the mothers the opportunity to be saved.

B) Father-son Banquet.

This would be similar to the mother-daughter banquet. However it could be more informal with possibly a cookout on a grille with a manly meal to encourage the dads to come. Honor the dads and share with them how important their responsibility is.

C) Parent Appreciation Banquet.

This is a great tool to reach parents. Have the young people put on a banquet for their parents. Make it a big event, with special music. Bring in a special speaker. Have the young people put on a skit and sing some songs. Present awards to some of the young people for Christian growth, soul winning, Christian character and faithfulness, Christian service award in the bus ministry, children's ministry, or for serving in the youth ministry. Present the award to the young person with their parents standing with them, and make it special, because it is special.

When inviting the parents to attend the banquet inform them that their son or daughter will probably be receiving an award. A good time to schedule these types of events is on Sunday afternoon about two hours before the evening service. This will be an encouragement for the parents to stay for the evening service.

Another very important thing to remember is to have "stand in parents". No matter what you try, some parents just will not come to anything. Do not leave any young person out, so have godly Christian people in the church be parents that day to stand in the gap and, make up the hedge for those young people whose parents refuse to attend. Grandparents can also be invited to the parent's banquet as well, but encourage the parents.

9) Be There When They Need you.

Always visit the family of your young people when a major event has taken place in their lives. Some events can provide the opportunity for you to share the gospel with them again. The following are examples of opportunities to visit the families of your young people.

A) A death in the family including grandparents, aunts, uncles and cousins.

B) Sickness in the family.

C) If you hear that they are going to move.

D) Dad or mom gets a job change or a job promotion. Stop by to congratulate them.

E) A Birth in the Family

Anytime the opportunity arises for you to build rapport, strengthen your relationship or lead them to Christ; take advantage of it.

10) Keep an Open line of Communication with Parents.

Always keep them informed of activities and events at the church. It is wise to send a brochure to the home of your young people regarding special activities, especially the ones that you may be charging money for. It is helpful to most parents if they know ahead of time for things they may need to help with financially.

Communications with the parents also shows them that you want their input, that you are organized, and that you are concerned about their young person.

Helping Young People Restore the Family

"So Abijah slept with his fathers, and they buried him in the city of David: and Asa his son reigned in his stead. In his days the land was quiet ten years. And Asa did that which was good and right in the eyes of the Lord his God: For he took away the altars of the strange gods, and the high places, and brake down the images, and cut down the groves: And commanded Judah to seek the Lord God of their fathers, and to do the law and the commandment. Also he took away out of all the cities of Judah the high places and the images: and the kingdom was quiet before him. And he built fenced cities in Judah: for the land had rest, and he had no war in those years; because the Lord had given him rest. Therefore he said unto Judah, Let us build these cities, and make about them walls, and towers, gates, and bars, while the land is yet before us; because we have sought the Lord our God, we have sought him, and he hath given us rest on every side. So they built and prospered."

II Chronicles 14:1-7

The family structure in America is in trouble. The divorce rate even among Christians is climbing. Then we have the thousands of couples who do not even take vows of marriage yet have several children. You may recall from the statistics in chapter one, the number of children who live without their biological fathers and the number of teenage girls who give birth to children each year out of wedlock is absolutely alarming. What can we do about the decline of genuine Biblical family values in America? How can we help this generation restore the family in America? How can we help young people who come from broken homes, and who have numerous family problems deal with their family problems and give them hope of a brighter future for family life? Allow me to share some Bible principles and thoughts on how we can help!

1) Assure them that God loves their family no matter what the condition of their family is.

After God created Adam and Eve and placed them in the Garden of Eden he blessed them. We read in Genesis 1:28 *"And God blessed them,"* The word *"blessed"* implies an act of adoration, an expression of love. God loved Adam and Eve when he created them, he loved them when he had good sweet fellowship with them in the garden and everything was well, and he loved them after they disobeyed him and ate from the forbidden tree. Dear friend, God loved them after they had disobeyed him enough to cover their nakedness, and he loved their descendants enough to give his only begotten Son to die for their sin. He loved Adam and Eve when they were in a sinless condition before their fall and he loved them as sinners after their fall, he loved them in either condition. God loves the Christian home with few problems and he loves the broken home that is lost without Christ and having numerous problems. He loves them both equally and He loves them both unconditionally. God loves the young person who has numerous family problems, with a dad that has left the home; the young person, whose mother never married his or her father. The young person whose dad is a drunkard or drug addict, whose mother is a prostitute with many "live in" boyfriends, needs to know that God loves his or her family just as it is. They need to know that God loves their family unconditionally.

2) Teach them what a Christian family is by example.

The only example of a Christian home some young people will see is when a Godly Sunday school teacher or youth leader invites them to theirs. One of the best things you can do to encourage a young person with family problems is show them what a Christian home is by inviting them into your home. Make them feel like a special guest, like "part of the family". Let them see that a loving Christian home is possible.

3) Encourage the young person with family problems to have a good testimony at home.

Just as God loves the family no matter what the condition of it may be, the Christian has a biblical responsibility in the home no matter what the condition of the home life may be. The youth leader must encourage the young person with family problems to do his or her very best to obey and honor their parents. The young person must show his or her lost parents that God is working, that God has made a change in their life and that they desire to please their parents.

Keep in mind that this may not be an easy task for the young person with serious problems in the home. They will need encouragement, strength, and assurance from their church and church leaders. They will need strong, concerned Sunday school teachers and youth leaders that will be willing to stand in the gap and make up the hedge.

4) Teach young people God's plan and purpose for courting, marriage, and children.

Although a young person may have family problems and come from a broken home, the important thing is that we encourage them that life does not have to continue on as such into their own adult life. We must encourage them that they can change things in their own marriages and family life; that they can break the family curse by making changes in their own families by setting goals and biblical guidelines for themselves. To accomplish this we must teach them Bible principles in the areas of courting, marriage and having a family of their own.

The following is a biblical formula to teach young people about how to restore the family and biblical family values in America.

A) Keep your purity for marriage.

B) Court only a believer of like faith.

C) Marry a person that shares the same biblical convictions and goals about the family that you have.

D) Develop a friendship with the person you want to marry.

E) Realize the importance of the wedding vows and the commitment and responsibility that comes with marriage.

F) Determine with your spouse that you are going to conduct your marriage and family according to the Bible and that you are going to serve God together.

5) Help young people with lost parents win them to Christ.

Take every opportunity to witness to the parents of young people that are in your youth ministry. Invite them to special services and church events. Take time to listen to them if they ever begin to open up to you. Exhibit a genuine concern for the parents and for their salvation. Encourage the young people to witness to their parents at every opportunity.

Getting Young People Involved in Church Ministries

"Then said I unto them, ye see the distress that we are in, how Jerusalem lieth waste, and the gates thereof are burned with fire: come and let us build up the wall of Jerusalem, that we be no more a reproach.

Then I told them of the hand of my God which was good upon me; as also the king's words that he had spoken unto me. And they said, Let us rise up and build. So they strengthened their hands for this good work."

Nehemiah 2:17-18

"And next unto him builded the men of Jericho. And next to them builded Zacur the son of Imri. But the fish gate did the sons of Hassenaah build, who also laid the beams thereof, and set up the doors thereof, the locks thereof, and the bars thereof." Nehemiah 3:2-3

If the Lord Jesus Christ tarries his coming for another generation, we must be involved in training the next generation for service. We must get our young people involved in the work of the Lord; in the preservation of the Word of God; in soul winning; and we must teach them that these things should be done through the authority of the local New Testament church.

Teenagers make a tremendous work force in the church when given proper motives, good leadership with the right attitude and a clear description of the purpose for the task.

1) How to get young people involved.

A) Leadership must see the need and the possibilities of meeting the need.

Leadership must realize the importance of training the next generation to be involved in the work of the Lord. Nehemiah assumed the position of leadership to get the job of rebuilding Jerusalem done. He led the people in doing the work that was necessary. He shared his burden and he set the atmosphere for the attitude of the workers.

B) Have a positive attitude about the work that is needed.

Remember one of the keys to being a success in leading people is that people will get excited about whatever leadership is excited about. If we want our young people to get excited about serving in a ministry of the church, then we must have a right attitude about the work that is to be done.

C) Present the need to the young people.

Nehemiah shared the need with the people he wanted to recruit to help him rebuild the walls. *"Ye see the distress that we are in, how Jerusalem lieth waste, and the gates thereof are burned with fire."* Your need may be for more workers in the bus ministry, or you may be encouraging your young people to get involved in soul winning. You may have a need to get the churchyard landscaped or to paint a Sunday school class. You may have an opportunity to have a nursing home ministry. Whatever the need may be, present it to your young people!

D) Share with your young people God's plan of meeting the need.

Nehemiah told the people, *"...let us build up the wall of Jerusalem, that we be no more a reproach."* Jesus presented a need to his disciples (and to us) in this manner; *"The harvest truly is plenteous, but the labourers are few; Pray ye therefore the Lord of the harvest, that he will send forth labourers into His harvest."* (Matthew 9:37-38) God's plan in meeting a need is prayer and action. Nehemiah prayed. He presented the need that was upon his heart to the king. He then presented the need to people that could help meet the need, and then they took action in doing the necessary work to fulfill the need.

E) Give everyone an opportunity to do something.

We can imagine that when Nehemiah and his men began to rebuild the wall some of the volunteers he had may not have been brick masons; some were probably not talented in the area of building; but they could assist those that were building. Let me say here that everyone can be a soul winner, however a brand new convert may need a little help. He may need to assist the experienced soul winner. Some of your work force may need to be silent partners, or assist the bricklayers. Some of your young people could visit the bus route while others could pass out flyers and help canvass a street for the bus route. Some can drive the lawn mower and some can rake the grass. My point is; everyone can do something, don't leave anyone out. Get all of them involved and help the one that can rake the grass learn to drive the lawn mower, and the one that is the assistant to the builder learn to become a builder.

F) Prepare them for service.

Teach your young people how to do the work, how to be soul winners, how to work the bus route, how to mow the grass.

G) Let them know what is required of them.

Tell them ahead of time how they should dress for the work they are to do. Advise them on what they need to bring with them, when to arrive and how to behave.

H) Let them know you appreciate their willingness and their labor and let them share in the harvest.

Thank them personally and publicly; award them for faithfulness and service. A little recognition with young people can go a long way in encouraging them and in helping you recruit more laborers.

2) Ministries teenagers can serve in.

A) The bus ministry

B) Junior church ministry

C) Soul winning

D) Nursing home ministry

E) Church cleaning, custodial work and maintenance

F) Decorating for special meetings, i.e. Revivals, Mission conferences.

G) Prayer Ministry

H) Ushering

I) Teenage girls can assist in the nursery, but should always serve as an assistant to an adult woman.

J) Teenage Choir or music ensemble. This is an excellent ministry to get teenagers involved in. You do not have to have a lot of musical ability to sing in a choir. Use these teen singing groups in your services, nursing home ministries, etc.

K) Visitation

Ministering to Young People in Public Schools

As a church youth ministry grows and develops it will have an increase in young people who attend a public school. These young people need to be encouraged, and they need to know that they are not alone as they strive to live for Jesus Christ and as they try to maintain a Christian testimony in a world of atheism, idolatry, and paganism as we have in our government schools today.

The public high school and junior high school in your town is a mission field and we can reach out to the students and administration, if we pray and use wisdom and compassion. We need to understand that the public school system is not our enemy, Satan is our enemy. The public school is a tool, a weapon if you will. The local church can disarm the enemy and have some influence in the public schools. We can use the weapon of the gospel and the power of prayer and influence to reach out to the young people in our public schools.

Consider these suggestions on how, as a local church, you can help your young people who attend a public school and how you can reach the other young people in the public school.

1) Pastor and or youth leader schedule an appointment with the school principal or administrator.

It is best for the youth leader and pastor to go together. If only one can go, it is wise to take another man along for support and to show the church's sincerity. The purpose of this appointment is not to tell the administrator all that he is doing wrong or how wicked the public school system is in your town. Your purpose is to offer your support and encouragement. No matter what we may think about the public school system in America, it is not an easy task for teachers and administrators to teach many of the students they have today, with the violence and lack of respect that exists among young people today. These teachers and administrators do not need our criticism as much as they need our encouragement.

2) Tell the administrator that you have several young people from your church attending the school.

Let the administrator know that you appreciate his and his faculties; efforts in providing an education and safe environment for the students. Express to him that you know how difficult his job must be. Let him know that you are willing to help in any way you can and that you want the teens in your church to be respectful toward school authority and to strive for excellence in their studies. Without mentioning any names, let him know that you have a few young people with family problems but that you are seeing progress in their lives and that you are encouraged by it.

3) Politely inform the administrator that you are going to begin meeting with your young people every Monday morning before classes at the school flagpole for prayer.

This is not something you need the school administrator's permission for, but it is something you could make him aware of if you are going to have a pleasant relationship with him. Let him know that you will be stopping by just for a few moments at the designated time to meet with your young people, to pray and encourage them to do their best that week.

4) Encourage your young people to meet at the flagpole each morning for prayer as a group.

They can have one lead in prayer or they can pray silently, but they should pray together each morning. The youth leader can encourage this by trying to meet them at the flagpole every morning for a week to help them get started and then to continue with them every Monday morning.

5) Have lunch with your young people in the public school cafeteria once a week or once a month.

You will also want to work with the school administrator on this as well. And to be honest, you may need his permission for this. Having lunch with your young people at their school is a great way to fellowship with them. You can also meet some of the other students and discretely invite them to a youth activity. A good way to enhance lunch time with your young people at their school is to order pizza from a local pizza place and have it delivered to the school cafeteria.

You can encourage your young people to invite some of their classmates to join them for lunch and to share in the fun and fellowship.

6) Organize a Public School Bible club in the local school.

This is a wonderful means of helping your own young people as well as a wonderful means of winning teens to Christ. The Bible club could meet one day a week after school for 30 to 45 minutes. A room in the school can be used for this. You can sing some songs, have games and skits and share a Bible message. The young people you have in your youth ministry can invite their classmates to participate. You can use the lunch time to promote the Bible Club. Get names and addresses of the young people who join the Bible club, the purpose of the Bible club is to win young people to Christ and to get more young people involved in your church youth ministry. Young people from other churches may want to be involved in the Bible club and that should be encouraged. However, it is best if you maintain control of the Bible club meetings and functions.

8) Bring in a School Assembly.

Granted that in this day and time it may not be an easy task to get the public school in your community to have a school assembly that you promote or endorse, but it can be done. Perhaps an Evangelist that preaches to teenagers, or a singing group that sings a lot of patriotic songs. Some evangelists have a public school assembly program on suicide, drugs, and violence, etc.... Such ministries can give you information on how to contact the school and how to make the necessary arrangements to schedule an assembly.

When I pastored in Ohio we brought in a singing group that had a public school ministry. They sang patriotic songs and had an anti drug message in their presentation. We were able to get them in three of the public high schools in our county. It was a blessing and many of the students who saw the assembly presentation attended the services we had in the evening.

The Pastor-Teenager Relationship

"And I will give you pastors according to mine heart, which shall feed you with knowledge and understanding."
Jeremiah 3:15

"He shall feed his flock like a shepherd: he shall gather the lambs with his arm, and carry them in his bosom, and shall gently lead those that are with young." Isaiah 40:11

Dear Pastor,

I don't have to tell you that you have a tremendous responsibility as a pastor of a local New Testament Church. You have a very important role in the lives of your young people. They need you! They need your involvement in their lives. They need your prayers, your leadership, your security, and your preaching. They also need to have a good relationship with you. I realize that you may have a full time salaried youth leader to "pastor" your young people. You may have godly and well-trained Sunday school teachers. You may have a fine layman youth leader over your youth ministry. That is all well and good, but your young people still need you. You are God's man! God has given you to those young people, *"And I will give you pastors according to mine heart."* You are their shepherd; you hold the highest office in the world. They need YOU!

Allow me to share some thoughts with you that can help you develop a good and an effective relationship with the teenagers in your church.

1) Love Them.

Love them as they are and encourage them to become great for the cause of Christ. Love them when they do right and love them when they stumble. Let them know that you love them; tell them from the pulpit; tell them in youth meetings; tell them one on one and tell them through your ministry.

2) Learn Their Name.

I realize that if you pastor a church of any size at all it sometimes becomes difficult to know everyone by their name; however people in leadership should try to know the names of their people. We should not only try to know their names but we should use their names when we are addressing them. People like to hear their name, especially by people in leadership.

3) Be Their Pastor.

As mentioned earlier, you may have a qualified youth leader that is doing an excellent job with your young people. But the young people still need you to be their pastor. When they have a need in their life, you should be involved in helping them with that need. When tragedy strikes, you should be there for them. Too often pastors get too busy for their young people, may I say, especially for the "bus kids". This should not be the case, let us remember that our Saviour said, *"Inasmuch as ye have done it unto one of the least of these my brethren, ye have done it unto me."*

4) Send Notes to Your Young People.

This is an excellent way to maintain some communication. You could write two notes a week or two a month if you have a very large youth ministry. Just a note of encouragement can make a big difference in the life of a teenager who may be struggling, or a "that a boy" note to the young person who may be striving to grow in the Lord and do great things for God. Your youth leader can help you with knowing who could use a word of encouragement from the pastor. I remember a letter I received from my pastor one time for something good someone had told him that I had done. He wrote to commend me for even a small task. That letter meant so much to me that I framed it and hung it on my bedroom wall. I still have it. A little edification can go a long way in building a relationship with young people.

5) Attend Youth Activities and Events.

Again, I realize that most pastors are very busy and have a lot going on in their churches, however it is encouraging for the young people to see their pastor attend or at least "stop by" for a few moments during a youth activity. For example, you could stop by long enough to pray with them before they go out on teen visitation. You could stop by the church to see them off as they go for an outing somewhere. You could stop by the miniature golf course during their golf outing. And for some activities you could spend time with them during the entire activity. And at some activities it is good for you to preach to them; to tell them that you love them and to share your vision for them, with them.

6) Talk to Them From the Pulpit.

It is good for the pastor to direct his attention to the young people while he is preaching to the entire congregation. Apply the truth you want to convey in your sermon to your young people. Statements like, "young people God has something for you" "teenagers don't let Satan rob you of your joy" "Young people hear me out." These types of statements help keep the young people's attention and let them know that their pastor is indeed preaching to them also.

When I was a teenager my pastor would sometimes preach directly to the teenagers for ten minutes or so during a sermon. He would get our attention by boldly saying, "You teenagers, sit up straight and listen to me tonight; you better be careful of the crowd you run with; you better leave the drug crowd alone; you better leave the rebellious crowd alone. Satan will use them to wreck your life." He, of course would be preaching to the entire congregation, but his attention would be directed to the teenagers. Other statements that are helpful to the young people and the youth ministry, is to make statements from the pulpit like, "We have the greatest young people in America right here in our church, and we had three people saved last week through our teen soul winning." Recognition for what they do right will give them a greater desire to continue doing right.

7) Personally Recruit Teens to Help in Needed Areas.

There is something about the pastor asking you to help him that gives a lot of young people a feeling of being important. I can remember as a teenager growing up at Emmanuel Baptist Church in Marion, Ohio when on several occasions my pastor called me to his office to ask me to help him with a project. Such as taking the bus attendance on Sunday morning as the buses enter the church parking lot. Or the time he asked me to help one of the men in our church paint the exterior of the building. It just helped me to know that he wanted me to do something for him, and the idea that he would personally ask for my involvement meant a lot to me.

8) Be Accessible.

Your teenagers should respect your position as their pastor; they should also respect the fact that you have a busy schedule; but they should also feel that you are accessible. They need the security of knowing that your door is open to them, and that they can come and talk to you about their life, their struggles, their victories, and the decisions they need to make in life.

9) Host a Youth Activity at Your Home for Your Teenagers.

As we previously mentioned, when you invite someone into your home, you have invited him or her into your life. It is helpful in developing a good relationship with your young people if you have them to your home at least once a year for an activity. You could host a Christmas party for them at your home, or a summer cookout. You can play a few games with them, fellowship, have fun, and share a message from the word of God with them. They will never forget those memories that you will make for them by taking the time to have them in your home.

10) Schedule a Personal Appointment with Them at the Beginning to Their Senior Year of High School.

This is a crucial time for young people; they have a lot on their minds; they are thinking of their futures and of some of the decisions they will be making about career and college.

During the appointment with them share some of the positive memories you have of watching them grow up in the church, commend them for the right things they have done. Share with them that you believe God has something special for them and that you believe they have a lot of potential. Ask them to tell you what their plans are and then listen when they talk. Tell them what you believe God has for them and what you see God doing in their life. Encourage them to attend a good Bible college if they have not already chosen to do so. Before you conclude the appointment tell them that you love them and pray with them. Let them know you are there for them.

11) Help Them Feel Like They are Part of Something.

The local church is one of the three greatest organisms in the world. The church is God's method of evangelizing the world. The Apostle Paul describes the church as a body in First Corinthians chapter twelve. For some teenagers the local church is not only a body of believers, it is the closest thing to a family they have. I have always liked the term, "church family" and I believe that a New Testament church should have a family atmosphere. As the pastor you help set the atmosphere of your church. To some people you a father figure. Like "Daddy" to a family, the one who provides security, the one who leads the family and trains them in the nurture and admonition of the Lord. Let your teenagers know you are glad they are part of the church family; always be glad to see them; cheer for them when they try; give them recognition when they achieve; lovingly reprimand them when they do wrong and encourage them to do right.

Preaching to Teenagers

"And he said unto them, Go ye into all the world, and preach the gospel to every creature." Mark 16:15

"For the preaching of the cross is to them that perish foolishness; but unto us which are saved it is the power of God." I Corinthians 1:18

"The Spirit of the Lord is upon me, because he hath anointed me to preach the gospel to the poor; he hath sent me to heal the broken hearted, to preach deliverance to the captives, and recovering of sight to the blind, to set at liberty them that are bruised, To preach the acceptable year of the Lord." Luke 4:18-19

"Preach the word; be instant in season, out of season; reprove, rebuke, exhort with all longsuffering and doctrine." II Timothy 4:2

As I begin to write this chapter I must confess that I am somewhat overwhelmed at the idea of writing on such an important topic as preaching. First Corinthians 1:21 says, *"...It pleased God by the foolishness of preaching to save them that believe."* The idea that God loves preaching and that Jesus Christ commanded the disciples to, *"Preach the gospel"* and that the baton of that command has been passed onto the preachers of today reveals to us both responsibility and opportunity. With those thoughts in mind allow me to make an attempt to share with you some thoughts about preaching to teenagers.

1) Pray about Preaching

E. M. Bounds said, "There can be no substitute, no rival for prayer; it stands alone as the greatest spiritual force, and this force must be imminent and acting." Prayer is the most important part of a preacher's ministry and if we are going to be effective in our preaching we must be on our knees often seeking the power of God for the purpose of preaching and meeting the needs of people.

A) Ask God to give you what your young people need.

There are times when they may need scolding, but there are other times when they need encouragement. Then there are times when they need to be challenged. Through prayer and in seeking the Lord concerning what is needed, the Holy Spirit will reveal to you what the specific needs of your young people are.

B) Pray for the filling of the Holy Spirit and for the power of God on your preaching.

C) Pray that you will be a blessing and not a hindrance.

D) Pray for wisdom in your preaching. You do not want to be offensive; you want to be helpful. Use humor with wisdom; raise your voice with wisdom and be blunt with wisdom.

E) Pray for compassion in your preaching and toward the people to whom you are preaching. They have needs; they have come to hear what you have to say; they want to hear what God has given you to give to them; deliver your sermon, with a heart of love and compassion.

2) Preparing Yourself for Preaching.

A) Prepare your Heart for Preaching.

This is a very important part in preparing to preach, and should include searching your heart and confessing any and all sin. It would also include a yielding of yourself to the Holy Spirit, a yielding of your heart, your mind and your thoughts. Consider the lives of the people to whom you are going to preach. Scan your audience. Look at the young people you are about to preach to. Love them and consider the needs they may have. Some of them may be going through a difficult time. Some of the teenagers you are going to preach to may have already written a suicide note. Some teenage girl may be close to giving up her purity, or may have already done so. There may be some teenager in your audience whose father has abandoned the family, or has abused them. They need something from the Word of God that is delivered from that man of God that has a genuine concern and love for them. Their whole lives may be before them or this could be the last sermon they will ever hear and it could be the last one you will ever preach. Have your heart prepared to share the message God has given you.

B) Focus your Thoughts.

Focus your thoughts on the importance and purpose of preaching. Focus on the power of the word of God from which you have derived your sermon. Meditate on the Bible truth that you want to project in your sermon, how that truth has helped you, and how it can help those to whom you will preach.

3) Preach the Word.

The Apostle Paul told young Timothy, *"Preach the word; be instant in season, out of season; reprove, rebuke, exhort, with all longsuffering and doctrine."* It is the preaching of the Word of God that can touch and change the hearts and lives of our young people. When we stand before them with Bible in hand we must proclaim it as truth. We must reprove, rebuke and exhort with all long suffering and doctrine. We must take every opportunity to help them from the Word of God. We must have the power of God on us and we must have compassion in our hearts. We must preach the Word, not new ideas, not philosophies, but the eternal Word of God. That is, "quick, and powerful and sharper than any two edged sword, piercing even to the dividing asunder of soul and spirit, and of the joints and marrow, and is a discerner of the thoughts and intents of the heart."

Preach a Hell that's hot and a Heaven that is sweet. Preach an enemy named Satan that seeks to devour and destroy their lives. And preach a friend and Saviour name Jesus Christ that gave His life and shed His blood on destroy their lives. And preach a friend and Saviour named Jesus Christ that gave His life and shed His blood on Calvary because He loves them and desires that they have life, abundant, victorious and eternal.

4) Meet Your Audience on Common Ground.

You are not better than they are and yet you are not their equal, you are the preacher. You have something on your heart that you came to share with them and to challenge and encourage their hearts. They have heartaches and you have heartaches. They have friends and you have friends, they have an enemy named Satan and you have an enemy named Satan. They will stand before God someday and you will stand before God someday.

They need Jesus Christ as their Saviour and you need Jesus Christ as your Saviour. Meet them on the common ground, but meet them as a preacher of the Word of God.

5) Use Personal Illustrations.

In preaching and in teaching I have found it helpful to use personal illustrations. Share illustrations using your family, your children and your parents. Share illustrations concerning problems you have had to deal with and decisions you have had to make in your Christian life; and what you learned about God's faithfulness, grace and power to help in times of need. Share your personal salvation testimony. That always makes an excellent illustration.

As a word of caution, be careful not to use illustrations about sin you may have personally been involved in. You do not want to give Satan any glory or portray the idea to teenagers that they need to go out and get into sin so they can have a "testimony". Also be careful with family illustrations in that you not embarrass your wife or children, which may cause you problems at home.

6) Present the Problem and the Solution.

I preach in a lot of youth rallies and conferences. I have preached with many good men over the years. However, I have seen some men get in the pulpit and preach against rebellion, drugs, alcohol, immorality, and gangs. Then they preach on how wicked everyone is that participates in such things, but by the close of their sermon they have not offered a solution. They never show the young person from scripture how to overcome those obstacles; how to have victory; or how to abstain from sin. They never give the solution to the problem.

When we stand before them with the gloom of the problems and evils in their world, in the end we must also point them to a Resurrected Christ, an empty tomb, and a Saviour that has overpowered death, Hell and the grave.

7) Make the Truth in Your Sermon Applicable.

As we previously discussed, preaching is presenting the solution to a problem. The next step then is to make the solution applicable. By this I mean we must not only tell the young people what to do, but we must give them the "how to do it". For example when I preach to young people about keeping their thoughts pure and having the mind of Christ, my outline would be something like this. (This is a skeleton outline; my actual outline would have more notes.)

I) What you put into your mind produces your thoughts, your emotions, and your behavior.

A) Satan is the father of all that is impure.

B) God is the father of all that is pure and right.

C) Jesus Christ wants us to think right so we can live right and honor him.

II) Things that produce impure thoughts

A) Satanic rock music

B) Immoral TV programs and movies

C) Gossip

D) Pornography in literature and on the internet.

E) Listening to dirty jokes.

III) The Christian is to have pure thoughts.

A) Thoughts about the goodness of God

B) Thoughts about the opportunities that God gives us to serve him.

C) Thoughts about bringing honor to the Lord.

D) Thoughts about winning the lost to Christ.

IV) How do we get our thoughts to be pure and Christ honoring?

A) Confess our sin of impure thoughts

B) Replace impure thoughts with thoughts that are pure and pleasing to the Lord.

1) Read the Bible

2) Memorize scripture.

3) Pray

4) Read good literature

5) Think about the needs of others.

6) Listen to Christ honoring music

C) Choose our friends carefully

D) Choose our thoughts carefully

E) When an impure thought enters your mind, confess, pray, and think of something good and pure.

Conclusion: You can change your thought life. You can keep your mind pure, you can keep your mind focused on the things of the Lord.

A) Ask the Lord for help

B) Commit to thinking pure thoughts

C) Get those things out of your life that hinder you from having pure thoughts.

D) Replace them with things that will help you keep your thoughts on pure and right.

With these points in my sermon I have tried to present the problem, the results of impure thoughts, the solution to the problem, and how to apply the solution to the problem.

8) Give Your Audience an Attainable Goal.

Ronald Reagan said, "I won the nickname, the 'Great communicator', but I never thought it was my style or the words I used that made the difference; it was the content. I wasn't a great communicator, but I communicated great things."

How well this statement describes an important aspect of preaching; the aspect of challenging and motivating people to move to action; to make victorious changes in their lives; to live for the Lord; to attempt big things for a big God. Preaching is indeed communicating great things, communicating Bible truths that can transform lives, and communicating goals. The Apostle Paul in His written sermon to the church at Philippi said, *"...forgetting those things which are behind, and reaching forth unto those things which are before, I press toward the mark for the prize of the high calling of God in Christ Jesus."* Communicating to young people the joy of living victoriously for our Saviour is an attainable goal and one that we should strive for. Challenging young people to rise above the status quo; to overcome life's obstacles, to put their hand to the plough, and press toward the mark. To give them a goal that they can obtain; to point them to the prize and then to cheer for them as they run the race. To remind them as Paul reminded the church at Philippi, *"I can do all things through Christ which strengtheneth me."* That is all part of preaching. Of course the greatest and most important thing to obtain is salvation through Jesus Christ. This is a goal that anyone can achieve by grace and through faith.

9) Be Personable

Your first time speaking to a group introduce yourself and give a brief biographical sketch of yourself. Share with your audience that it is your honor and privilege to be with them.

10) Keeping the Teenagers Attention during the Sermon.

The most important part of any speech is the introduction. Those first thirty seconds of your sermon are crucial in capturing your audience's attention. Consider the following thoughts about keeping your audience's attention.

A) Begin with a welcome and expression of gratitude.

I want my audience to know that I am pleased to be with them and that I am pleased that they are in the meeting.

B) Announce that you have something important to share with them.

Everything in the Bible is important, so express that you need and desire your audience's attention. What you have to say will help them; what you have to say may be life changing and you want their undivided attention.

C) Use your voice to keep your audience's attention.

There are times when delivering a sermon that it is wise to raise your voice to stress a point, and there are other times when it is better to lower your voice to stress a point. The preachers voice should fluctuate when preaching, do not speak in a monotone.

D) Don't stand in one place.

I realize that it may not be everyone's "style" to walk around the platform or in the audience while preaching. However, I have found that in preaching to teenagers it helps keep their attention if you do not stand in one place. I also believe that when you walk out into the audience you are putting yourself "among them" so to speak.

E) Don't push your audience's time and attention limit.

There is an expression that professional sales people use, "Don't talk yourself out of the sale." I realize that preaching is not selling, but there is a truth in that expression that can apply to preaching. The point is that the preacher should not over extend his audience's attention span. There is only so much people can retain and if you try to preach through the whole Bible in one setting you may "talk yourself out of the sale". In other words, your presentation may be good, but you did not make a conclusion to the point, you did not get them to the place of decision.

It is best to share one great Bible truth in a sermon. Encourage and challenge your audience with that Bible truth, bring your sermon to its climax and then stop. Don't go back and rehash everything again and again; go to the decision making time; proclaim your call to action. And then shut up!

The Bible truth you have proclaimed is now in the hands of your audience. Let them do something with it.

11) Preach on Topics that Teenagers can Relate to.

When I preach in a juvenile prison, I do not preach on the topic of, How to be a good student in a Christian school. That would not be a topic that my audience could relate to and it is not a topic that would meet their need. Neither would I preach in a Christian school on, How to survive in prison. Before I begin to study and prepare for my sermon I need to be praying about what the needs of my audience is. I also need to know my audience. The preacher that preaches to teenagers should know something of the issues teenagers deal with in our society. They should know what the biggest temptations and trials are that teens deal with today.

Remember that preaching is giving solutions to problems, so we must be aware of what the problems are so we can present the solution with wisdom and compassion. When I have a possible mixture in my audience of teenagers whose parents attend church regularly and another population in my audience who have only been to church a few times or possibly this is their first time; in my message I must challenge and encourage each group represented. I must encourage the teenager whose mother is addicted to cocaine while also challenging the teenager with Christian parents not to become rebellious. I must express grace to the teenage girl who has lost her purity and is heartbroken over it, while preaching against fornication to that teenager in my audience who is on the edge of losing her purity. I must preach hope to the teenager whose father has abandoned him or her, while preaching on honoring your parents.

I must preach on topics that my audience can relate to. I must give them Bible solutions to questions they have as teenagers. I must get across to them that God has balance in an unbalanced world. I must, through preaching the Word of God, bind up the broken hearted; proclaim liberty to the captives; give beauty for ashes; joy for mourning and praise for burdens.

The Following is a list of topics and subjects that I think are important to preach on to teenagers.

1) Salvation

2) Peer pressure, how to deal with it

3) Dating-courting

4) The Bible and the future

5) The Bible and current events

6) God's solutions to life's problems

7) God's promises to man

8) Finding God's purpose in life

9) How to make life better

10) How to deal with family problems

11) Forgiveness

12) Heaven

13) Hell

14) How to live a victorious Christian life

15) How to trust God in difficult times

16) Stewardship

17) Success

18) How to make the right decisions in life

19) Why we believe what we believe

20) The Bible

21) Love

22) Perseverance

23) God's love for us

24) Fundamentals of the faith

25) Standards

26) Drugs

27) Alcohol

28) Gangs

29) Missions

30) Soul winning

31) Our relationship with others

32) Our relationship and responsibility toward parents.

33) Obedience to those in authority

34) Family

35) Living in the will of God

36) The preservation of the Local Church

37) The preservation of the Bible

38) The preservation of the family

12) Give an Invitation

As we have discussed preaching is giving a solution to a problem; it is challenging and encouraging people to serve the Lord more; to be more faithful and it is rallying Christians to the cause. This being the case at the close of each sermon it is decision time or may we say, "call to action" time. We are given a good example of sermon delivery, presenting the problem, the solution and the charge to make a decision in Joshua's last sermon to the Children of Israel in Joshua chapter twenty-four. Joshua reminded the people what God had done for them, how He had brought them out of bondage and into the land of Canaan. Then he challenged them in verse fourteen, *"Now therefore fear the Lord, and serve him in sincerity and in truth: and put away the gods which your fathers served on the other side of the flood, and in Egypt; and serve ye the Lord."* Then Joshua gave the call for the people to make a decision in verse fifteen, *"And if it seem evil unto you to serve the Lord, choose you this day whom ye will serve;"* The invitation in Joshua's sermon was to decide to serve the Lord.

The invitation does not begin at the close of the sermon. For example, Joshua's invitation actually began when he called all the children of Israel to Shechem. The sermon invitation begins when people walk into the room where the sermon will be preached. The invitation begins with the welcome, the song service, the handshaking time, the opening prayer, the sermon introduction and the sermon. All of these things are part of the invitation; the climax of the invitation is at the close of the sermon. The actual invitation is a very important part of any service. It is the time designated for encouraging people to do business with God, to respond to the preaching of the Word of God. Hebrews 10:23-25 says, *"Let us hold fast the profession of our faith without wavering; (for he is faithful that promised); And let us consider one another to provoke unto love and to good works: Not forsaking the assembling of ourselves together, as the manner of some is; but exhorting one another: and so much the more, as ye see the day approaching."* Notice the words in verse twenty-four; *"let us consider one another to provoke unto love and to good works."* The word *"consider"* means to look at with attention, to perceive. The word *"provoke"* means to stir to action. The invitation is a time in which people are given to look at their lives and examine their hearts with attention. It is a time to examine their relationship with Jesus Christ. The invitation is a time to be stirred to action, to respond to the leading of God. I personally believe that each time the Word of God is preached an invitation should be given for people to take action and do business with God at an old fashioned altar.

Helping Teenagers Develop Camaraderie

"Let us hold fast the profession of our faith without wavering; (for he is faithful that promised); And let us consider one another to provoke unto love and to good works:

Not forsaking the assembling of ourselves together, as the manner of some is; but exhorting one another: and so much the more, as ye see the day approaching."

Hebrews 10:23-25

It seems that with all of the teen violence, crime and suicide in our society everyone is looking for a way to improve the lives of our young people. Our federal and local governments and public schools have offered everything from midnight basketball, to mentoring programs and the distribution of free condoms. None of these "programs" and "quick fix" ideas have lowered our crime rate, or slowed down our teen pregnancy problem or fixed anything else for that matter.

I don't know of anything more effective and productive than a local New Testament Church having a youth ministry that reaches out to teens and others with the gospel; offering wholesome activities and teaching Biblical values and character while preparing them for adulthood. Our young people need to develop wholesome Christian friendships. This is especially important for those who have troubled family lives. Christian young people who develop relationships with others their own age that share the same Biblical values, convictions, purpose, common goal and love for the Lord Jesus Christ will be less likely to meddle with the lures of the world. I believe there are some principles and practices we can implement in our youth ministries that can help our young people develop friendships and relationships that will last them a life time.

1) We Share a Common Bond

As born again believers in Jesus Christ we have a common bond in that we are born into the family of God. We are going to spend eternity in Heaven. We are united in Christ. A common bond builds camaraderie.

2) We Share a Common Purpose

God has created everyone for a purpose. No one is an accident. God brings us together for a purpose. As born again believers united in the same local New Testament Church we share a common purpose. That primary purpose being to glorify the Lord Jesus Christ through winning souls, edifying one another, and discipling new converts! A common purpose builds camaraderie.

3) We share a Common Need as Believers

Romans 14:19 instructs us, *"Let us therefore follow after the things which make for peace, and things wherewith one may edify another."* We need edification; we need to be built up, and encouraged in the Lord by our fellow Christian friends. It is not easy for young people to live for Christ in this world today. So it is important that we teach them and give them the opportunity to edify one another. A common need builds camaraderie.

4) We Share a Common Command

We are commanded in Hebrews 10:25, *"...exhorting one another:"* To exhort is to invite or to entreat. As fellow Christians we should exhort one another to good works, to be faithful, to persevere when difficult times come along. To press toward the mark. Exhorting one another builds camaraderie!

5) One Accord in Prayer

In Acts 1:14 we find the believers at the local New Testament church, *"These all continued with one accord in prayer and supplication..."* When the power of God fell on the church at Jerusalem three things were in place; One, they were in agreement (one accord), Two, they were in the same spiritual condition (one place) and Three, they were in prayer. Prayer accomplishes so much that I do not know where to begin, except to share these few thoughts. Prayer forces us to get our hearts right. Prayer develops concern for one another. Prayer places us in the presence of God. Prayer helps us do what we cannot do on our own. Prayer involves God in what we are doing and prayer builds camaraderie. I challenge you to get your teenagers praying for one another and get them praying together before each service at your church. Have the girls meet in one room to pray and have your young men meet in another room to pray together for thirty minutes before each service. Watch God do a work in their lives and in your church. Charles G. Finney said, "Every great movement of God has been started by teenagers." I warn you to be careful, as you may have a revival breakout as a result of your young people praying.

6) Let us Labor Together in a Common Work

Nehemiah said *"So we laboured in the work."* Referring to the rebuilding of the walls of Jerusalem in Nehemiah 4:21! Work is pleasure not punishment, it should not be looked upon as something we have to do but as something we get to do; sspecially the work we do for the Lord like soul winning, visiting our bus routes, or preparing for a youth activity. Getting our teenagers involved in laboring together through the local church in the work of the Lord will build camaraderie among them.

7) Let us Care for One Another

We live in a society in which the mentality is that the government is supposed to care for all of our needs. However, the Bible teaches that Christians are suppose to care for one another. Several scriptures come to mind concerning this topic.

"...forgiving one another" Ephesians 4:32

"abound in love one toward another."
First Thessalonians 3:12

"comfort one another" First Thessalonians 4:18

"edify one another" First Thessalonians 5:11

"exhort one another" Hebrews 3:13

"consider one another" Hebrews 10:24

"Speak not evil one of another" James 4:11 "Confess your faults one to another" James 5:16 "and pray one for another." James 5:16

Simply put, we should teach our young people to care for each other; to encourage and help each other through good times and bad times; to be concerned for the lamb that strays away and to cheer for the one that returns home.

We are in this world together until the Lord comes for us, so let us care for one another. Caring for one another builds Camaraderie!

Church Teens and Bus Teens

Some pastors and church leaders get nervous when we talk about infiltrating the "Bus kids" and the "Church kids" into one group. I have had some pastors even tell me that they did not want anything to do with the bus ministry because they did not "want the bus kids to mess up their good church family kids". How sad this kind of thinking is, that a minister of the gospel would lack vision and compassion for the lost.

To be blunt about the matter I have seen "good church family kids" mess up some bus kids. I believe we lose many of our bus kids because we do not include them in the church youth ministry and involve them in the ministries of the church.

Allow me to share some observations on how to merge the two groups and as you read these thoughts it is important that you keep two things in mind. One, I realize that not everyone will agree with me on this issue. Secondly, what you have read so far has been written by a "bus kid" who very strongly believes that the bus ministry is still one of the most important ministries for the New Testament church today. And that it is a means of, reaching multitudes with the gospel of Jesus Christ.

1) Leadership is Crucial

The leadership in the church must have a burden and desire to reach lost and un-churched teenagers. Leadership must relay that burden and desire to the people of the church including the teenagers.

2) Attitude is Crucial

Leadership must portray a right attitude toward the teenagers and children brought in on the buses. The young people who ride the bus are not a lower form of life. They mostly come from homes that do not know Christ and many of them have problems in their families. They need to be born again, they need to be loved and they need to be accepted.

They need a church that will love them as they are and see them becoming all that they can be for Christ. Who knows, some of them may even grow up and be preachers and write books.

3) The Church Youth Ministry Should Reach Out to all Teens Including, "Bus Teens".

Include bus teens in all church and youth activities even if you have to make special arrangements for transportation. A teenager that rides the bus on Sunday morning is not disqualified from attending the services on Sunday night and the fact that he or she rides the bus Sunday morning should not be a hindrance to him or her becoming involved in other church activities. One of the best ways to "fire up" the Sunday night service is to have a large number of teenagers sitting in the front section of the auditorium to hear the preacher "cry aloud and spare not".

4) The Local Church is One Body with Different Members.

"But now are they many members, yet but one body."
I Corinthians 12:20

"That there should be no schism in the body; but that the members should have the same care one for another."
I Corinthians 12:25

Church leadership must teach by example to the young people the importance of the local body of believers working together in serving the Lord. Each member has its work to do and assignment in the body, so the bus teenager is just as much a part of the body as the rich teenager and the church teenager from a Christian home.

5) Treat them Fairly.

"God is no respecter of persons;" Acts 10:34

"...unto whomsoever much is given, of him shall be much required;" Luke 12:48

Realistically more should be required of the church teenager than the "bus teenager" because he has received more. We do not expect a new convert to know as much of the Bible as the pastor knows and we cannot expect the young person that is a new convert to behave the same way a young person from a Christian home behaves. We cannot expect any young person to be perfect. We just expect them to be growing spiritually from where they are.

6) The Blood of Jesus Christ makes us all Equal.

Where they come from does not determine their present spiritual condition. Their walk with God determines that. I have seen some bus teens that were more spiritual than teens from some Christian homes.

7) Get the "Church teens" involved in the bus ministry.

One of the best things you could ever do for a "church teen" from a fine Christian home, with loving parents and far more material things than they really need is to take them to visit a child that lives in a rundown house, with a drunkard mother, no dad and very few material things. Then ask that teenager if he understands what the Bible means when it says, *"Jesus was moved with compassion when he looked upon the multitude."*

Be careful about taking the "church teen" to visit a new "bus teen" that lives in a bad situation. The "bus teen" may be embarrassed by his peer seeing his living situation so it is better to take the teenager to visit a younger child, not his peer.

8) Teach your mature Christian teenagers to express grace to new teens and "bus teens".

It is only by the grace of God that the "church teen" is not a "bus teen". The roles could be reversed.

9) Teach mature Christian teenagers to be an example of the believers.

Mature Christians have a responsibility to reach out in friendship and Christian brotherhood to every believer no matter how they got to the church house.

10) If given the opportunity, most young people will reach out to each other.

Teenagers will usually work out their differences when given a common goal and when all are made to feel important by those in leadership.

11) Solid Bible preaching will balance differences.

Preach the word of God strongly and compassionately to all the teenagers without categorizing them based on where they came from. Focus on what God wants of them now, and where they came from or how they got to church on Sunday morning will not be the primary issue.

The Teen Soul Winning Ministry (Personal Evangelism)

"The fruit of the righteous is a tree of life; and he that winneth souls is wise." Proverbs 11:30

"And Jesus came and spake unto them, saying, All power is given unto me in heaven and in earth. Go ye therefore, and teach all nations, baptizing them in the name of the Father, and of the Son, and of the Holy Ghost: Teaching them to observe all things whatsoever I have commanded you: and, lo, I am with you alway, even unto the end of the world. Amen." Matthew 28:18-20

The Great Commission was given to the Local New Testament church; it has been passed down to us through the perpetuity of the church. Going soul winning is one of the key assignments given to the local church. Soul winning is a command given to every born again believer, personal soul winning is not a calling, it is a command, it is not a leading, it is a command, it is not a gift, it is a command. If we are going to further the gospel onto the next generation, we must teach them the importance and the command of the Great Commission in the area of personal soul winning.

One of the most important reasons to have a local church youth ministry is to teach young people how to be soul winners.

The following are some principles on how to implement a teen soul winning ministry.

1) Soul Winning is Exciting.

As I have quoted several times already, "people get excited about whatever you are excited about". In order to motivate your young people toward soul winning, it is important that the leadership get excited about soul winning. Soul winning is helping meet mankind's greatest need, the need for a Saviour. Soul winning is pointing people toward Heaven so that they can avoid going to Hell for eternity. Soul winning is introducing people to the best friend they could ever have, the Lord Jesus Christ. Soul winning is giving people the knowledge that God loves them; that they are important to God; that he has hope available to them and that God wants to give them eternal life. Soul winning is what God commanded every believer to do. Soul winning is very dear to the heart of God. SOUL WINNING IS EXCITING!

2) Organizing the Teen Soul Winning Ministry.

A) Be First Class.

Soul winning is the business of the King of Kings and Lord of Lords and thus the pastor and youth leader should be organized, possess a good attitude about soul winning and make all necessary preparations in organizing and administrating the soul winning ministries of the church.

B) Have a Designated time to go.

Of course every Christian should take every opportunity to share the gospel with people they come into contact with, but it is also effective if we have a designated time in which we *"Go ye therefore"* to share the gospel of Jesus Christ.

C) Take a Step by Step approach to establishing a teen Soul Winning ministry.

There are several effective ways to get your teenagers involved in soul winning. You could begin by taking a teenager soul winning with you. That is something that can be done on a regular basis as a means of going soul winning and spending time with your teenagers individually to develop a personal relationship with them. However to establish a teen soul winning ministry that will grow; get teens excited about soul winning and get them winning souls to Christ, consider the step by step approach.

Step One: Training.

Your first teen soul winning meeting would include training on how to be a soul winner. I would recommend spending thirty to forty-five minutes on how to approach a prospect.

Step Two: Begin simple and work your way up.

If your teenagers have never been soul winning before, you will not want to force them to eat steak if they have not yet had milk. An effective way to help them start soul winning is to have them take a gospel tract or John and Romans and a Church flyer and simply say to the person who comes to the door. "Hello, my name is Don Woodard, this is Joe French, we are from the Central Baptist Church youth ministry and we wanted to give you a gift." As they hand the literature to the person at the door. The next statement they would make is, "Thank you for your time, and have a good day." This is a simple thing that anyone can do. There is usually little rejection if any at all.

Step Three: Share the Gospel

Once you have gotten your teens comfortable with the idea of knocking on doors or stopping people on the street and talking to them; and after a little more training on how to actually win a soul to Christ; have them go out and share the gospel with others.

3) Preparing for Soul-Winning.

A) The Soul Winning meeting.

Before going out soul winning meet with your teenagers. Share soul winning procedures and training. Have some of your teens do a soul winning practice drill. Ask for testimonies about a soul winning experience. Recognize those who are new to soul winning and those who have grown in their soul winning efforts.

Give a Bible challenge on soul winning. Have a time of prayer asking the Lord to prepare the hearts of the soul winners and the hearts of those with whom you will be sharing the gospel.

B) Items Needed.

A pocket New Testament, 3x5 cards, gospel tracts with the church's name and phone number on them, breath mints.

C) Attire for Soul Winning.

Neatly dressed, no baggy pants or shirts for the young men, but neatly "tucked in" shirt tails and modest clothing. Dresses or skirts for the young ladies, we want to represent our Saviour well. Shoes shined, hair combed neatly, young men should be clean-shaven.

4) Approaching the person to whom you will witness.

A) Go in Pairs of Two.

It is not wise to send a teenager out alone to knock on doors or to witness to people in unfamiliar territory. Jesus sent the disciples out in twos and going soul winning with a partner has some advantages. One does the talking while the other one is the silent praying partner. Two people arriving together at a home to share the gospel gives the purpose of soul winning more authority, urgency and importance than one person does.

B) The Introduction.

Introduce yourself, your partner, state the name of the church you are with and your purpose. For example, "Hello, my name is Don Woodard and this is Joe French, we are from the Beacon Baptist Church youth ministry on Sandy River road. We are out talking to people today and wanted to introduce our church to you. Do you folks attend church anywhere?"

C) Build Rapport.

After introducing yourself, your partner, your church and your purpose and have asked if your prospect attends church, let them respond and begin to build rapport. Find something for which to make brief conversation. Compliment them for attending church or if they do not attend church invite them to attend your services Sunday.

D) Ask them about their Salvation.

You can do this by asking, "Sir, I appreciate your time and courtesy to us, and it is good to know that you attend church. I am thankful for my church as well. However the most important thing is that we know for certain that we are going to heaven when we die. Sir, do you know for sure that you would go to heaven if you were to die today?" Or you could ask this way, "Sir, I appreciate your time and courtesy, may I ask you this, If you were to die today do you know for sure that you would go to Heaven?" If they answer that they do not know, begin to open your New Testament and ask, "Sir may I show you from the Bible how you can know that you will be in heaven for eternity?"

E) Explaining the plan of Salvation.

1) Romans 3:23 *"For all have sinned, and come short of the glory of God;"* "Mr.______, this simply means that we are sinners. We were born sinners. I have sinned against God and you have sinned against God. We have done things that displease him; we were born with a sin nature. Mr.______, would you agree with the Bible that you and I have sinned and that we are both sinners?"

2) Romans 6:23 *"For the wages of sin is death; but the gift of God is eternal life through Jesus Christ our Lord."* Mr.______, because we are sinners and because sin has a penalty we are going to die someday! The word death here is separation; sin separates us from God. If we die without Jesus Christ as our personal Saviour we will go to hell and we will be separated from God for eternity. Notice the end of the verse says, *"...the gift of God is eternal life."* God offers eternal life to us through His Son Jesus Christ.

3) Romans 5:8 *"But God commendeth his love toward us, in that, while we were yet sinners, Christ died for us."* Mr.______, In spite of our sin and sin nature, God loves us. He expressed His love to us through Jesus Christ, God's only begotten Son dying for our sin on the cross. Jesus Christ paid our sin debt; He paid the penalty for our sin at Calvary. Jesus Christ purchased eternal life for us on Calvary, eternal life in Heaven is free to us because Jesus Christ paid a great price for it on our behalf. He shed His blood, took the punishment of our sin and died for our sin.

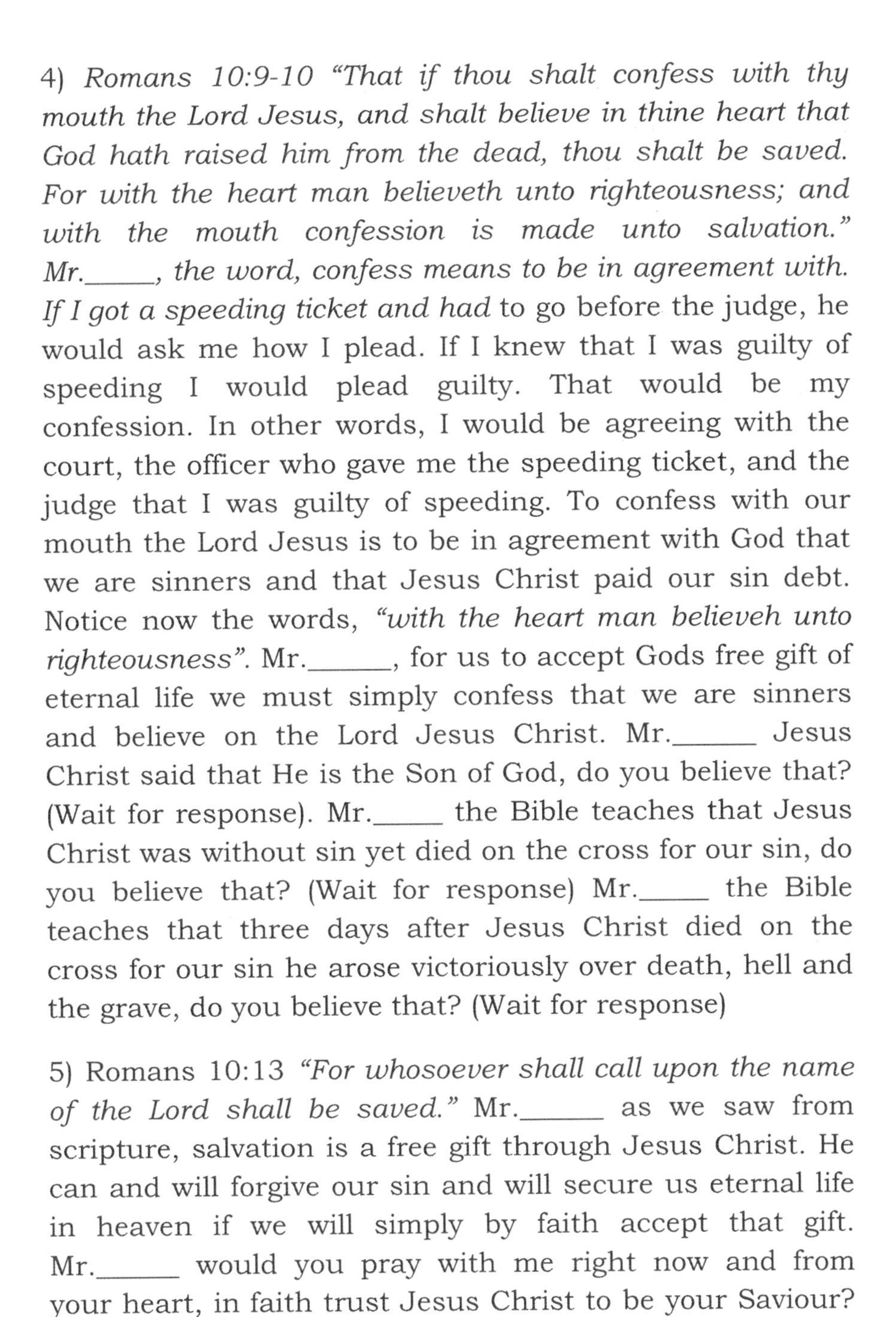

4) *Romans 10:9-10 "That if thou shalt confess with thy mouth the Lord Jesus, and shalt believe in thine heart that God hath raised him from the dead, thou shalt be saved. For with the heart man believeth unto righteousness; and with the mouth confession is made unto salvation." Mr._____, the word, confess means to be in agreement with. If I got a speeding ticket and had* to go before the judge, he would ask me how I plead. If I knew that I was guilty of speeding I would plead guilty. That would be my confession. In other words, I would be agreeing with the court, the officer who gave me the speeding ticket, and the judge that I was guilty of speeding. To confess with our mouth the Lord Jesus is to be in agreement with God that we are sinners and that Jesus Christ paid our sin debt. Notice now the words, *"with the heart man believeh unto righteousness"*. Mr.______, for us to accept Gods free gift of eternal life we must simply confess that we are sinners and believe on the Lord Jesus Christ. Mr.______ Jesus Christ said that He is the Son of God, do you believe that? (Wait for response). Mr._____ the Bible teaches that Jesus Christ was without sin yet died on the cross for our sin, do you believe that? (Wait for response) Mr._____ the Bible teaches that three days after Jesus Christ died on the cross for our sin he arose victoriously over death, hell and the grave, do you believe that? (Wait for response)

5) Romans 10:13 *"For whosoever shall call upon the name of the Lord shall be saved."* Mr.______ as we saw from scripture, salvation is a free gift through Jesus Christ. He can and will forgive our sin and will secure us eternal life in heaven if we will simply by faith accept that gift. Mr.______ would you pray with me right now and from your heart, in faith trust Jesus Christ to be your Saviour? (Bow your head) Mr._____ pray something like this from your heart, "Dear Lord, I know that I am a sinner, I believe

that You love me and died for all my sin, I ask that You forgive me of my sin and I now trust You to be my Saviour. Amen"

6) John 3:36 *"He that believeth on the Son hath everlasting life:"* Mr.______ you have believed on the Son of God. He said he would give you eternal life if you would believe on Him. God always keeps his Word; God has given you eternal life in Jesus Christ by his grace and through your faith.

7) John 10:28-29 *"And I give unto them eternal life; and they shall never perish, neither shall any man pluck them out of my hand. My Father, which gave them me, is greater than all; and no man is able to pluck them out of my Father's hand."* Mr.______ God has given you eternal life because you asked Him for it in faith, nothing or no one can take that from you, and God will not take it from you either. It is eternal; that means it is yours forever.

After the person has been led to Christ get their full name and address for follow up later. Invite them to the next church service.

This is a skeleton overview of leading someone to faith in Jesus Christ. I recommend that you teach your teenagers a more detailed soul winning course. There are several good books on soul winning. Dr. Curtis Hutson's *The Soul Winning Kit* is an excellent tool for teaching soul winning, as is Dr. Shelton Smith's video set titled, *The Soul Winning Church.* Choose a good soul winning course, learn it, then teach it, and then put it into practice. Teenagers can be a wonderful workforce in the local church, especially in the area of soul winning.

Increasing Your Teen Attendance

"And the lord said unto the servant, Go out into the highways and hedges, and compel them to come in, that my house may be filled." Luke 14:23

Step One: Pray

Prayer should be at the forefront of any and all ministries in the Local church. Through prayer we should always be seeking guidance and power and we should be praying for all of the young people in our care

In beginning a campaign to win teenagers to Christ, and increase the teen attendance in our church we should begin by praying earnestly for the Lord's help. Not only should we be praying ourselves but we should enlist prayer partners to pray with us and for us; not necessarily people you can meet with every other day for prayer. I'm talking about people who will pray for you, your teenagers, and the teen ministry as you try to reach more teenagers for Christ.

So the first step toward increasing your teen attendance is PRAYER!

Step Two: Become A Servant

The Bible tells us in Philippians 2:7 that Jesus, *"... took upon him the form of a servant, and was made in the likeness of man:"* We hear a lot about leadership today, it seems that everyone is having conferences on leadership, and these are good things. However, I fear that we have forgotten to be servants. The key to becoming a good leader is in learning to be a servant to those whom we serve. As a youth leader we are to serve our teenagers and their parents. If we are going to increase our youth ministry, reach more teenagers, and become more effective in their lives we must ask ourselves how we can serve them! How can we help them deal with life's issues? How can we help them make the right decisions in their lives? How can we protect them? In leadership we often think of Jesus feeding the five thousand and we want to have that experience in our ministry. But we forget that when Jesus was alone with the twelve disciples, he washed their feet. He was a servant. If you want to be a leader of a multitude of teenagers, learn to be a servant to a few.

Step Three: Plan

Begin with making a list of activities you would like to have over the next six months. Plan one big activity per month. Plan what you are going to be teaching in the Sunday school classes. Plan a promotion and visitation program. Go over your plan with your pastor, ask him for advice. Plan your work and work your plan. Stick with your plan, stay faithful.

Step Four: Take Inventory

There are two important things one must know when taking a journey. We must know the starting point and the destination. A business in order to be successful develops a plan. The plan always includes inventory. Having the knowledge of what is in stock and what needs to be ordered is important to any business. In developing a more effective youth ministry and increasing that youth ministry, we must know what we have in inventory, we must know where we are starting from and what our destination is. The following is an inventory check list.

1) What is my personal spiritual condition?

2) What is the spiritual condition of my young people?

3) What is my relationship with my young people?

4) How well do I prepare for my task each week for the Lord?

A) Lesson preparation!

B) Study preparation!

C) Prayer preparation!

5) What resources do I have access to that could help me serve better?

A) Ministry related books

B) Periodicals

C) Cabinet of counselors: Fellow youth leaders that I can call for advice.

6) Who is on my team?

A) The Pastor, fellow laborers, people who could help with the youth ministry.

7) Who is on my Roster?

A) Current young people I am ministering to.

B) How well do I know them individually?

C) What are their needs?

D) Who are my current prospects?

8) Action to take:

(Example)

Do I need to be more devoted to my personal devotions? Do I need to strive to be more prepared? Should I Pray more for my young people? Should I visit more? Should I spend more time with my family?

Step Five: Get Excited!

Your attitude will be reflected in the attitude of your young people. If you will get a good Biblical positive attitude about the things of the Lord, your church, the opportunity to serve the Lord, and to work with teenagers, your teenagers will get excited about the same thing. As a successful Christian businessman shared with me when I asked him what he attributed his success to he stated; "I figured out that people will get excited about whatever you are excited about!"

This is a powerful truth if you will get a grasp of it. Teenagers will get excited about whatever you are excited about. So—get excited about reaching more teenagers. Get excited about every church service and every opportunity to serve the Lord. Get excited about learning the Bible and get excited about soul winning. Get excited about seeing teenagers live victoriously for God and your teenagers will get excited about it too! If the leadership gets excited about the possibilities of reaching teens and having a growing productive teen ministry, the rest of the Church will get excited about it too!

Remember—Excitement and a right attitude breeds excitement and a right attitude and contentment breeds contentment!

Step Six: Make a Prospect List

Making a list of prospects to contact for your teen ministry is not as complicated as you might think if you know where to look. Begin with the teenagers you currently have. Give each of your teens a sheet of paper, ask them to write their name and phone number at the top of the sheet, then ask them to list the names of three teenagers they know who may or may not attend church.

Your next step would be to schedule a time that each of your teens can go visit the prospects with you. I suggest that you have a "special service" or a planned activity you can invite the teens to.

The second place to get prospects is from the adults in your church. Do any of your adults have teenage grandchildren, neighbors, or other contacts which may have teenagers that may be prospects you could make contact with?

What about the Sunday school teachers who teach the younger children? Do any of those younger children have older teenage brothers or sisters? Get a list from them and visit every prospect inviting them to attend a service or special teen activity.

Always be prepared when you meet teenagers in the highways and hedges; keep a pocket notepad to write down names of teenagers you meet. Keep your card and youth ministry flyers available to pass out. Every teenager you meet is a prospect for your teen ministry. You will find that as you begin to make contacts, a network begins. This person knows that person and this teenager has these friends and so on. There are twenty seven million teenagers in America and my guess is that a couple hundred of them live in your community.

Step Seven: Visit Every Prospect

Make contact with teens! Communication is important! Visit every prospect you get. Introduce yourself to the teenager. Be excited to meet them and be excited about the teen ministry of your church. Give them your card, phone number, and information about your teen ministry. If they don't attend after your first visit, then visit them again. In sales they say, "Every prospect is a prospect until they buy or die." We are not trying to sell anything, we are giving it away. His name is Jesus. He loves teenagers. He wants to give them abundant life and we are His servant, sharing with others what He wants to do in their lives. We should work harder than a salesman promotes his products. We have an opportunity to touch the future of America. Every teenager is a prospect, and we have to visit all of them.

Step Eight: Get the Word Out

Promote your youth ministry, get some cards printed with your name, your teen ministries name and phone number on them. Have a brochure printed up explaining the teen ministry. Detail what you are about, the activities and services you have available to teenagers. Keep a supply of the brochure on hand then get them to the bus workers, the pastors, and anyone who may come into contact with prospective teens. Also keep activity flyers printed up about upcoming events. Take them to teen hang outs; put them up where ever teens may see them. These things are easily made on a computer. It should become natural to the youth leader to pass out flyers and information about the teen ministry.

Step Nine: Teach a Topical Series

Teenagers do have questions about life and about the future and current events. I suggest that Sunday school teenagers and youth leaders teach on issues and topics that are important to teenagers, topics that concern them. Sometimes it is wise to take a topic of interest and teach a series on it in Sunday school. Make it interesting and as you visit prospects tell them about the series, share with them the interest of the topic. For example: A series could be taught on; What does the Bible say about war? What does the Bible say about the world ending? What does the Bible say about the future?

A six week series on these kinds of topics in a youth ministry growth campaign can be very helpful. It will help develop interest and can be used as a focal point to draw young people to the Lord and into the church.

I suggest that before teaching any series you get your pastor's approval. Another suggestion I would like to share is that I encourage every pastor to take two Sundays a year and teach the teen Sunday school class. He could teach on his vision for this generation or, What God says about your life! Or, God wants you to win! It would be an encouragement to the teens and would give them an opportunity to get to know the pastor. Of course this could also be done on special youth activities.

Step Ten: Have One Big Activity A Month

It is important to provide good wholesome activities for teenagers. In doing so you will accomplish several things! A monthly activity teaches them that Christians can have fun and you will also give them the opportunity to develop camaraderie among themselves. You give them something to look forward to and an activity is an opportunity to get lost teenagers to hear the gospel.

The monthly activity should be well planned, it should be promoted well, and it should be prayed over. Plan the activity in advance; many teenagers work today so it is helpful if they can know when to ask off of work for a teen activity. Know exactly what you are going to do, set the time, the place, and the focus. Make the activity evangelistic, use every opportunity you can for your teens to bring visitors, and use every opportunity to share the gospel.

Every activity does not have to be entertaining; some activities should be for serving the Lord. You can have a work day at the church. Activities do not need to be costly, you can plan picnics where everyone brings a sack lunch and you just play some games. Activities can be used to promote bringing visitors and an award can be given to the teen that brings the most visitors.

Step Eleven: During A Promotion Present Awards Publicly

If you are going to organize a six to twelve week campaign to increase your teen attendance, include awards that can be earned by your teens for bringing visitors. The award can be something as simple as a gift certificate to a pizza place. The award is not as important as the recognition and appreciation for a job well done. However, a nice gift is certainly appreciated by the teenager. Present the award publicly. I suggest in the Sunday evening service. I also suggest presenting one to a boy and a girl. There are several ways you can do this, you can give an award to the teen boy and girl who bring the most visitors to Sunday school three weeks in a row. It keeps the momentum going if you don't go any longer than three weeks, because at the end of every three weeks everyone has a fresh start.

During a campaign you could give an award to the boy and girl teens that bring the most visitors to the monthly teen activity as well.

Step Twelve: Maintain Constant Communication with Your Teens

We live in the era of communication, it seems that everyone has a cell phone and everyone has e-mail. The wise youth leader will use these things to his advantage. You can begin by making a list of your teenagers' e-mail addresses. You could basically send them an e-mail note daily, perhaps with a brief devotional. Get their cell phone numbers, call them every week! If they are struggling with something, call them more often. (Not all teens are on the internet so ask them how active they are on it if you are going to be e-mailing them).

Visit your teenagers! I cannot tell you how vital this is, even if you have to visit them at their job. Visit all visitors ASAP! Visit all prospects and follow up with them. If you are consistent in visiting them they might get the idea that you care about them and want to help them through their teen years.

Send them notes, as we mentioned you can send many of them e-mail notes. But touch base with them from time to time with a hand written note. Let them know you are praying for them, let them know you are glad they are part of your teen ministry and that you believe God is doing great things in their life.

Step Thirteen: Invest Time with Individuals

Someone has wisely said, "The best way to reach the multitude is to meet the need of the individual." This is what Jesus did. We read in Matthew 4: 23-25 about Jesus going into the various towns teaching, preaching and healing people of their infirmities. The scripture says that the sick were brought to Him. In verse 25 the Bible says, *"And there followed him great multitudes."* The multitudes followed Him because He met the needs of the individual.

If you are going to increase your teen ministry, meet the needs of the individual, invest in the individual. Invest your time, show an interest and help them with their individual problems. Don't scold them all the time, if they are having trouble they don't need you to ride them, they need you to show a concern. Make an investment, it will pay huge dividends!

Step Fourteen: Sunday Night Teen Time

"Teen Time" is a concept I would like to get every church in America to do and for several reasons. One: it gets more teens to Sunday night church. Two: it gives the more teens the opportunity to hear the pastor and get to know him better. Three: it shows the teens that the church cares about them. Four: it shows teens that God's people can have fun.

So what is "Teen Time"? Teen Time is simply a 30 to 45 minute activity held for the teenagers every Sunday night after church. It consists of a short Bible message, a skit, a few games and some refreshments. It is very easy for a church that has its Sunday night service at 6:00 PM to do. Keep in mind that most teens are going to stop by for pizza or hamburgers after church anyway, so why not control that time? Why not invest in them during that time? Why not use it as an opportunity to have an influence on them?

You can give different people an opportunity to share a Bible message with them. For example, any visiting missionary or evangelist, layman in the church, the pastor can be a frequent speaker, this gives him the opportunity to share his heart with his teenagers and encourage them. It can be a time for the pastor to get to know the teens and for the teens to get to know the pastor.

If a youth leader builds excitement about the Sunday night Teen Time, it can be very effective in increasing the teen attendance of the church and can also be used as a tool to reach parents.

Step Fifteen: Recruit Workers

As the church teen ministry begins to grow, the youth leader will need to recruit some workers to help with activities, to help with communication, and to act as chaperones. So allow me to make a few suggestions. First of all pray and ask the Lord to give you some good people to be on your team in the youth ministry. Secondly, before you ask anyone to help, clear if with the pastor, ask if he could suggest someone or ask if he thinks the person or couple you have in mind would be suitable. It is best to recruit a married couple if at all possible. It should be a couple who have an interest in teenagers, and will respect the idea that you are the leader serving the teenagers under the authority of the pastor and you need them to assist you on your team.

In recruiting a couple you may want to begin by inviting them to assist you with one activity. After they get an idea of what you do and what the youth ministry is all about, then ask them if they would consider being an assistant

Boy Friend Girl Friend Relationships

I have decided to include this topic because I am often asked about my views concerning teenage dating, teens going steady and courtship. The following are some guidelines and thoughts concerning boyfriend, girlfriend relationships in the local church youth ministry.

1) The pastor and youth leader must determine and set the standards and the attitude about boyfriend, girlfriend relationships within the church youth ministry.

2) Bible preaching and teaching on the subject of proper relationships between young men and young women should be done frequently. The Bible principles that it is not good for a man to touch a woman; that sex is for marriage, and that the decision of whom to marry is one of the most important decisions in life should be taught and preached on. That purity is a gift you give your spouse on your wedding day is a good way to help teenagers focus on remaining pure.

3) It is not wise for the church leadership to encourage teenagers to practice the concept of "going steady". First of all "going steady" is not a biblical teaching. Secondly it causes problems within the youth ministry.

Girls and boys sometimes begin to compete for relationships with different ones to go steady with. It puts a focus on which boy or girl a teenager is having a relationship with instead of how their relationship with the Lord is growing. It often builds tension, strife and division between teens and then sometimes the parents even get involved. Thirdly, to "go steady" with someone requires a commitment to the person you are going steady with, that commitment usually requires a token of the commitment such as the exchanging of class rings or other items. This often leads to one of the parties (usually the boy) wanting a further commitment, and a more personal token of that commitment. When a commitment is made between two people the idea is present that the person who has made the commitment is obligated to prove their commitment. In essence this too often leads to fornication, pregnancy, and broken hearts.

4) "Going steady" also leads to breaking up.

This leads to a bad habit that often follows a young person into adulthood. A young person "goes steady" and "breaks up", "goes steady" and "breaks up", "goes steady" and "breaks up", gets married and gets divorced, gets married and gets divorced, gets married and gets divorced. This seems to cheapen what a relationship between two people should be; people are not automobiles that we trade off when we tire of them. Our young people should be taught that a relationship between a man and a woman in marriage is precious and special. And the person one chooses to marry should be done prayerfully and delicately.

There are also emotional consequences involved in the practice of "going steady". Each time a boy or girl makes a commitment to someone of the opposite sex and stays committed to that person for any length of time they become attached emotionally and in doing so they give a little piece of their heart to that person. If a girl goes steady with Bill and Sam and Joe and Jeff and Dan and Steve and then later on marries Phil, she has given pieces of her heart to six other young men. On her wedding day to Phil, six other young men have a piece of her heart. It is far better that we teach our young people the importance of waiting on the Lord for the person God has for us. That we prepare ourselves and keep ourselves physically and emotionally pure for the one we marry.

5) "Dating" for church activities.

On occasion you may choose to have an activity such as a banquet for your young people. For such events some of the young people may wish to have a "date". To keep from making who is going to the banquet with whom the primary focus of the banquet it is better to use terminology such as "accompany" instead of "date". For example instead of making it an issue of "who is your date" or "I need a date". The young men can simply ask a young lady to accompany him to the banquet (after he has obtained permission from the young lady's father and / or the pastor). There is far less commitment and stress involved in accompanying someone to a banquet than there is being or having a date!

6) Courtship.

The concept of courting is biblical. A young man and a young lady spend time with each other after obtaining permission from their parents to see if there is a possibility of a serious relationship. In courting no commitments are made, no items are exchanged, and nothing is required from either party except that they be kind to each other and respectful of one another. It is my opinion that young people should not get involved in courting until they are out of high school.

Keeping Teenagers after Graduation

"Yea, and all that will live godly in Christ Jesus shall suffer persecution. But evil men and seducers shall wax worse and worse, deceiving, and being deceived. But continue thou in the things which thou hast learned and hast been assured of, knowing of whom thou hast learned them; And that from a child thou hast known the holy scriptures, which are able to make thee wise unto salvation through faith which is in Christ Jesus." II Timothy 3:12-15

There are five major events that take place in people's lives that trigger change in their habits, their thinking, and their life style. The first is a drivers license, the second is a first job, the third is High school graduation, the fourth is marriage, and the fifth is the birth of their first child. After any major event in life we often change lifelong habits and graduation from high school brings on many changes in the life of a young person. After graduation many young people feel that they have more freedom than before; they no longer have to answer to schoolteachers; they are experiencing adulthood like never before; and they have achieved an important accomplishment; one that they had worked toward for twelve years. It is time to move on to bigger and better things, so they may think. The local church needs to make every effort to keep young people involved in being faithful to the Lord and in seeking His will and direction for their lives. As well as remaining involved in the local church. The following are some suggestions on how we might better accomplish this.

1) Take every opportunity to encourage young people to full time Christian service. Of course we realize that the Lord is not going to call every young man to be a pastor, evangelist or missionary, and He is not going to call every young lady to marry a preacher or be a missionary. However, every Christian should be in "full time" Christian service. We should all be involved in soul winning, serving in the church in various ministries and that should not change after graduation.

2) Commend your graduates for their accomplishment of graduating from high school and encourage them to pursue the things in life that they believe God has called them to.

3) Encourage the graduate to go to a fundamentally sound Bible college for at least one year. This will give the opportunity for the young person to experience some independence while still under the influence of Christian leadership. This also helps give them the opportunity to make a clear decision on what to do with their life if it has not already been determined. Going to a good Bible college also helps them reach a higher level of their potential.

4) Get your young people involved in a ministry in the local church while they are still in high school. In the chapter on getting teens involved in church ministries several ideas are shared on areas of service such as Sunday school, Bus ministry, building and maintenance, nursing home, ushering.

5) Teach young people that with more freedom, more knowledge, more maturity and more blessings; comes

added responsibility. We read in Luke 12:48b *"For unto whomsoever much is given, of him shall be much required: and to whom men have committed much, of him they will ask the more."* The young people have learned how to live through the local church, now they have responsibility in the Local Church. They have been taught Bible principles of victorious living, now it is time to give back. The Lord has been faithful to them; they are to remain faithful to Him.

6) Build strong character in them while they are young.

7) Have a Sunday school class for high school graduates to get involved in immediately after graduation. This will be very important for all graduates, as they do not yet fit in the adult arena of life and yet they have risen to a new level of adolescence. This class would be for college and career aged young people and it should have a dedicated teacher that is concerned for helping his pupils grow in the Lord as they venture out into adulthood in search of living their dreams and ambitions. Consider these thoughts on helping young people make the transition into the college and career class.

A) Have the teacher send a letter upon graduation inviting the graduate into the class.

B) Have an activity for the graduates after graduation to congratulate them and to welcome them into the college and career class. A meal at a nice restaurant would be appropriate with the pastor attending the activity as a special guest to speak to the entire class.

C) The college and career class should have a ministry in the church that they are responsible for which the new class members can become a part of.

D) The college and career class should have their own soul winning time as a class.

E) The college and career class should have monthly activities.

F) The college and career class could correspond with the young people who have moved away to attend college in another town. Sending cards and care packages will be helpful to college students who are away from home. Reading letters during Sunday school from out of town college students will help keep the class informed and concerned for the young person who is away.

8) The pastor should have a personal meeting with the young person before they graduate from high school. This was discussed in the chapter on The Pastor Teenager relationship; it is mentioned here as a reminder.

9) Visit any of the recent graduates any time they are absent from a service. They need to know that just because they have graduated from High school nothing has changed. They are still expected to be in church when the doors are open.

Results of Survey Taken among Pastors

As I prepared to write this book I sent out a survey to several pastors, some of which I know personally and others that I am familiar with. Each of these pastors, I feel have very successful and effective youth ministries in their churches.

I wanted to share some of the questions I asked them, the answers they gave and the ideas they shared. The survey was mailed to twenty pastors and twelve of them responded.

I'm certain you will find their answers and the information obtained from the survey helpful.

1) Do you have a paid staff youth leader or a volunteer layman?

Four Pastors reported that they have a volunteer layman youth leader while eight reported a full time paid staff youth leader.

2) Do you have a weekly soul winning ministry?

All twelve of the pastors surveyed, who I remind you have effective youth ministries, have a weekly teen soul winning ministry.

3) What have you implemented in your teen ministry that you feel has helped to increase your teen attendance?

"Teens in action faithfulness program."

"Wednesday night teen Bible study, activities monthly, involving them in church activities."

"Five Sunday morning teen van routes"

"Sunday school contests involving teens in ministry, and special outreach activities"

"Soul winning"

"Activities and teen visitation."

"Youth Leader, Bus ministry"

"Organized activities and bring a friend night"

"Visitation of teens"

"Youth fellowships"

"Having a meal after soul winning which is just before the Wednesday evening service."

"Teen van routes"

4) What do you feel helps your young people grow the most spiritually?

"Companionship and doing things together with other Christian teens."

"Personal Bible study, inner growth as a priority of life."

"Preaching"

"Preaching, personal devotions and serving God"

"Soul winning"

"Solid Bible teaching"

"Preaching, Christian school"

"Teen devotions and involvement in church ministries"

"Teaching and preaching from the word of God, interaction with godly men and women"

"Prayer, Bible study, Bible teaching, opportunities to use what we have learned."

"A combination of soul winning, the youth activities and the preaching in the services."

"Being part of the *Young Fundamentalist* program which requires faithfulness to all services and participation in every other program that pertains to teens. Soul winning, activities, camp, youth conference, teen revival."

5) Does your church youth ministry have a weekly teen meeting?

All twelve pastors reported that their teens do have a weekly teen meeting. However, two of them considered the teen Sunday school meeting as the teen meeting.

6) Does your church have one big activity a month for teens?

All twelve pastors surveyed reported that they have one or more monthly activities for their teenagers.

7) Do you take your teens to an annual Bible camp or youth conference?

Eleven of the pastors surveyed said they do take their teens to an annual Bible camp or youth conference. The pastor, who said he does not, has several splendid youth meetings throughout the year. I have preached for this particular pastor three times and I know firsthand that he has an outstanding youth ministry in his church.

8) As a pastor do you have an annual meeting with your high school seniors to discuss the plans they have for their future?

Ten of the pastors shared that they do have a meeting with their high school students before graduation. One pastor shared that his youth leader meets with his seniors.

9) Does your church have a Bus Ministry?

I am pleased to report that all twelve pastors surveyed are in the Bus Ministry.

10) What advice would you give to a pastor who wanted to reach out to the teens in his community but cannot afford to pay a full time youth leader?

"Many pastors have led the youth ministry themselves. This would be a wise thing in this situation, since the pastor would be in close contact with a group that needs much guidance and can give much support."

"Make it a priority. My first added staff member when very strapped for money was a combination music/youth man." (This pastor has one of the most effective youth ministries in America)

"Have a heart for your youth. Teenagers can tell when you are just 'doing it.' Give of your time to do something on a consistent basis, even if it is only once a month."

"Have a youth night, keep it spiritual but show them love."

"Try to develop a great relationship as their pastor, be accessible to them."

"Use a good layman that loves God and teens."

"Recruit and train good lay leaders, have exciting activities, and make them feel loved and welcomed when they come."

"Be personally involved in their lives. Have fun with them, and give them personal attention."

"Find a good layman to work with your teens. Have a good evangelist come in and excite the church for youth ministry."

"Be much in prayer that God would send you a man whose heart is for teens and not just a stepping stone to the pastorate. Make full use of your facilities."

WHAT IS
"TEENS OF AMERICA"?

Teens of America is a ministry designed with the intent of reaching teenagers through assemblies / seminars held in public schools. Please don't let that fool you! Though we use the technique of public speaking to public school teenagers, we want to reach teenagers for Christ! Our primary goal is not to be a drug, alcohol, and crime prevention program. We firmly believe that drugs and alcohol have destroyed many young people's lives, but our desire is to win them to Christ and see their lives changed!

TEENS OF AMERICA
Evangelist Sean Mulroney
P.O. Box 1035
Arnold, Mo. 63010
636-299-6220
sjmulroney@teensofamerica.net
www.teensofamerica.net

Also by: Dr. DON WOODARD

Teenager, You Can Make It!..........................$5.00

When The Will of God is a Bitter Cup:
Healing for the Broken Hearted..................$11.00

Blessings from Parenthood.........................$5.00

Marrying the Right One.............................$7.00

161 Fun Games for Christian Young People..$5.00

Sermon on CD:
Six Things Muslims Teach their Children........... $6.00

Dr. Don Woodard
LightKeeper Publications.com
PO Box 490
Troutville, VA 24175
540-354-8573